Choices

Perspectives of Gay Men on Monogamy, Non-monogamy, and Marriage

Blake Spears and Lanz Lowen

www.thecouplesstudy.com

ISBN-13: 9781536890792
ISBN-10: 1536890790

Book and cover design: Brad Reynolds: www.integralartandstudies.com

Introduction

This is a compendium of two studies, and a follow-up article. The first study in the compendium is the most recent (2016). Simply called **Choices**, it focuses on monogamous and non-monogamous male couples. It is followed in this compendium, by **Beyond Monogamy**, which was conducted in 2010. *Beyond Monogamy* focuses solely on the experiences of long-term non-monogamous male couples.

The catalyst for both studies was our experience as a long-term gay couple. We had been together in a non-monogamous relationship for 36 years and were curious about the experience of others. There wasn't any roadmap and we assumed long-term couples might offer valuable perspectives and hard-earned lessons. We took several years interviewing 86 long-term non-monogamous couples. We shared what we had learned in *Beyond Monogamy* on our website (www.thecouplesstudy.com) and received positive feedback about the usefulness of the information. Six years after posting the study, we are still receiving 50 hits a day and Beyond Monogamy is being downloaded 40 times per month. This speaks to the lack of information about non-monogamous gay couples.

Having completed *Beyond Monogamy*, we embarked on another study, this time seeking out the perspectives of younger gay men (under 40 years old). Because we were hearing the younger generations were more inclined toward monogamy, we made this a study of monogamy, non-monogamy, and marriage. Again, we heard diverse perspectives, but we also found trends towards greater monogamy and the emergence of "monogamish" relationships. We called this study *Choices* since it provided insights, profiles and descriptions of both monogamous, as well as non-monogamous male couples.

In addition to the two studies, we are including an article that was written as a follow-up to Beyond Monogamy. *Creating Healthy Open Relationships*, focuses on the elements of successful relationships and discussion of some of the typical issues that couples encounter (jealousy, conflict, trust). The examples are of non-monogamous couples from our 86 interviews. Although it is aimed at non-monogamous couples, the principles and suggestions would also apply to monogamous couples.

We hope you find this information helpful. Our intent is to reflect back to the community descriptions of the wonderful diversity found in male couples. Whether monogamous, monogamish, or non-monogamous, we found many examples of strong, healthy and loving relationships, from which we can all learn.

You can find *Choices*, starting on Page One. *Beyond Monogamy*, follows, starting on Page 101. The article, *Creating Healthy Open Relationships*, begins on Page .

Table of Contents

Chapter 1
Study Methodology and Demographics

Overview

In a previous study we interviewed 86 long-term male couples who were in mutually consensual non-monogamous relationships. The purpose was to describe what 'successful' non-monogamy might look like and to identify helpful behaviors, mechanisms, and perspectives. Because we required couples to be together 8+ years, couples skewed older, with the average age being 50 years old.

This current Study targets gay men from 18 – 40 years old. We've enlarged the scope of the Study to include monogamous, as well as non-monogamous couples, in order to get more data about preferences of respondents in this age group. Although most of the questions and focus are on respondents who are currently coupled, we also polled younger single men on certain questions, particularly those pertaining to preferences for monogamy or non-monogamy.

Study Objectives

- Identify the prevalence and attitudes about monogamy and nonmonogamy in the younger gay male population
- Describe existing monogamous and non-monogamous couples in terms of viability, relationship health, what works and what's challenging
- Identify to what degree gay marriage is desired by younger gay men and the degree to which marriage is associated with monogamy
- Provide findings that bring greater awareness and information to younger generations of gay men as they make decisions about their relationships

Methodology

The study consisted of two different online surveys and 30 telephone interviews.

Quantitative Survey

- Initially, we conducted an online survey which we advertised on Facebook in September, 2014. (See Quantitative Survey Questions in the *Appendix*). The Facebook referrals came from diverse parts of the USA, both urban and small town environs and their responses served as our primary quantitative data. We had the following respondents in the FACEBOOK COHORT:
    - Singles — 242
    - Monogamous Couples — 290
    - Non-Monogamous Couples — 48
- Since we had so few non-monogamous couples respond to the Facebook ad, we also, placed an ad in Grindr (a gay male sex hook-up app) in late September, 2014. We had the following respondents in the Grindr COHORT:
    - Singles — 328
    - Monogamous Couples — 42
    - Non-Monogamous Couples — 79
- Because we assumed that the Grindr audience skewed toward non-monogamy and the population was urban (Seattle, San Francisco, Portland) we were selective about how we used the data. We added the data from non-monogamous couples responding to the Grindr survey to data from non-monogamous couples responding to the Facebook survey for purposes of better understanding non-monogamous

couples. This gave us 127 non-monogamous couples. We purposely omitted the data from Grindr singles and monogamous couples in most of our analysis.

Qualitative Survey

- As we were analyzing the Facebook and Grindr data, we noticed there were a significant number of couples who described themselves as monogamous, even though they had 'threeways' and/or occasional sex with 'outsiders.' We were curious about this, and decided to conduct a second survey in October, 2014. The survey, which primarily consisted of open-ended questions (See Qualitative Survey Questions in the *Appendix*), was conducted online using a FACEBOOK advertisement.

- In this survey we only enlisted participants who were in relationships (no singles).

- We instructed participants to identify as:
  - Strictly monogamous
  - Monogamous, but held 'loosely'— 'monongamish'
  - Non-monogamous

- We had the following number of respondents:

  - 632 monogamous couples, of which 161 completed the written comments
  - 152 'monogamish' couples, of which 45 completed the written comments
  - 48 non-monogamous couples, of which 16 completed the written comments

- Participants answered the open-ended questions that pertained to their 'orientation toward monogamy.'

Interviews

- We conducted follow-up interviews with 30 respondents that volunteered by self-identification at the end of the second Facebook survey. Interviews averaged 30 minutes and provided us with additional examples, perspectives and the ability to profile a small number of couples. We interviewed:

  - 15 participants involved in a monogamous relationship
  - 5 participants involved in a 'monogamish' relationship
  - 10 participants involved in a non-monogamous relationship

Study Population

Number of Respondents	Quantitative Study	Qualitative Study
Single	242	N/A
Monogamous	290	632
Non-monogamous	127*	48
"Monogamish"	N/A	152
Total	576	853

*Includes Grindr cohort

Number of Respondents with Written Comments

Number of Respondents	Quantitative Study	Qualitative Study
Single	N/A	N/A
Monogamous	N/A	161
Non-monogamous	N/A	16
"Monogamish'"	N/A	45
Total	N/A	222

Age Range of Quantitative Study Respondents
(n=576)

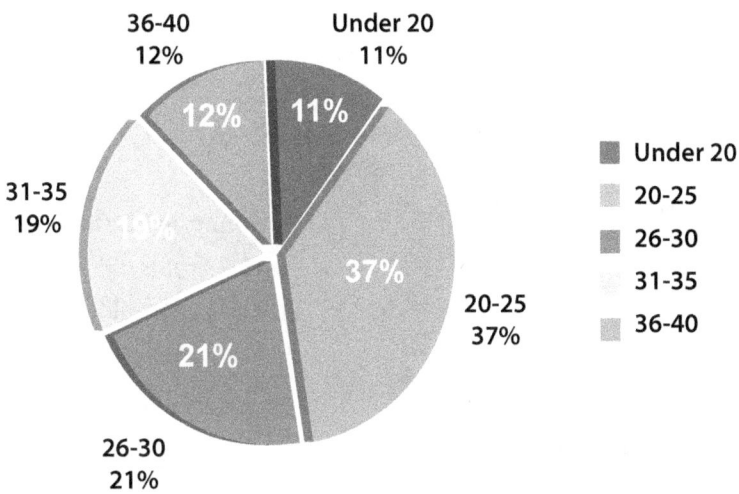

36-40 12%
Under 20 11%
31-35 19%
20-25 37%
26-30 21%

- Under 20
- 20-25
- 26-30
- 31-35
- 36-40

Ethnicity of Quantitative Study Respondents
(n=576)

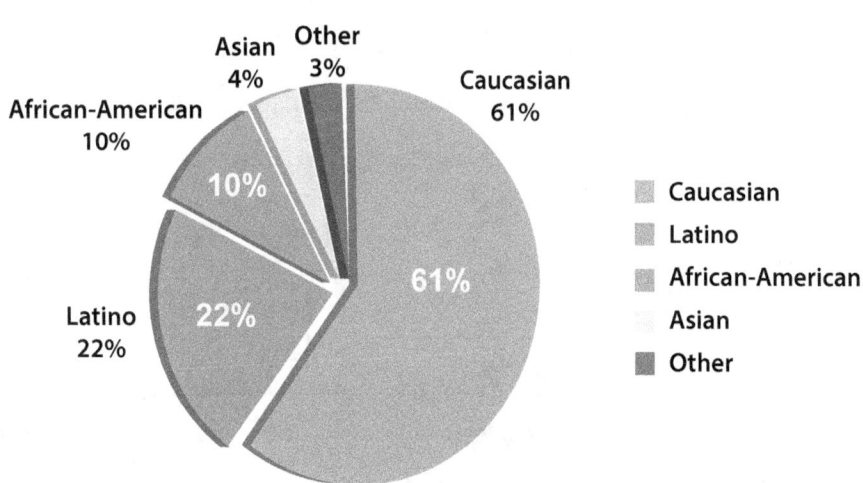

Asian 4%
Other 3%
Caucasian 61%
African-American 10%
Latino 22%

- Caucasian
- Latino
- African-American
- Asian
- Other

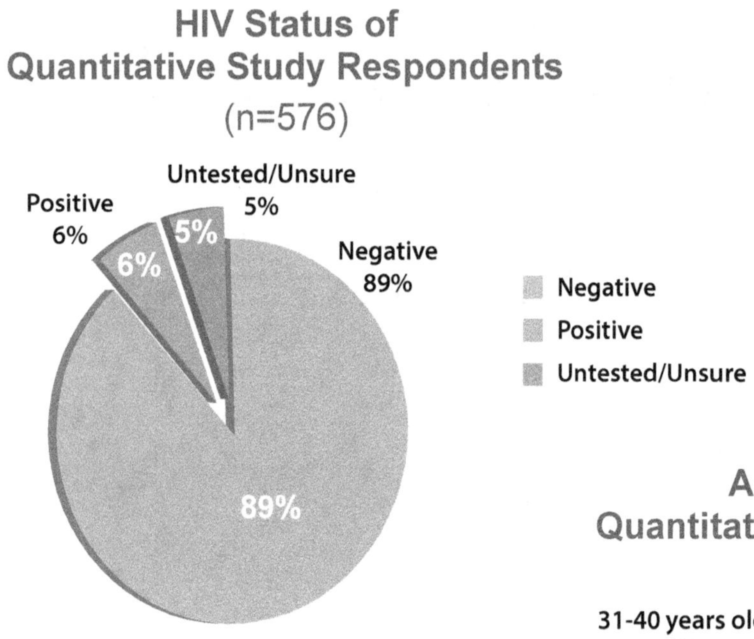

HIV Status of
Quantitative Study Respondents
(n=576)
Untested/Unsure
5%
Positive
6%
Negative
89%
6%
5%
89%
Negative
Positive
Untested/Unsure

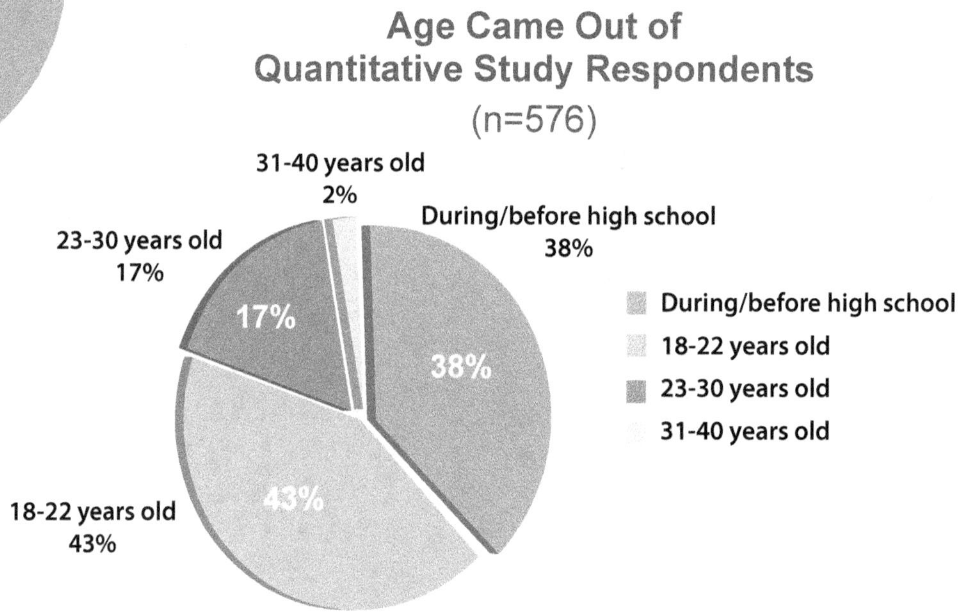

Age Came Out of
Quantitative Study Respondents
(n=576)
31-40 years old
2%
During/before high school
38%
23-30 years old
17%
17%
38%
43%
18-22 years old
43%
During/before high school
18-22 years old
23-30 years old
31-40 years old

Length of Relationship of Quantitative Study Respondents
(n=417)
%
60
50
40
30
20
10
0
49%
28%
29%
30%
22%
42%
2 years or less
3-5 years
6 years or more
Monogamous
Non-monogamous

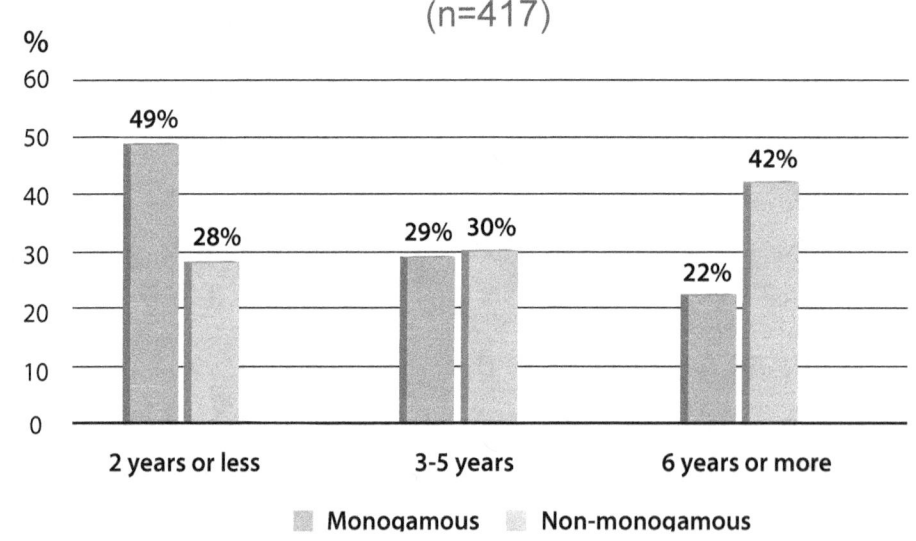

Study Highlights

- Younger generations seem more inclined toward monogamy than their elders.
  - In our quantitative study where all of the participants came via FaceBook, 42% of respondents were single; 50% of our respondents were in monogamous relationships; 8% of our respondents were in non-monogamous relationships.
  - Of the single respondents, 90% stated they were seeking monogamous relationships.
  - Research conducted by others characterizes almost half of long-term gay relationships as non-monogamous (Shernoff, 2007). *See Page 7.*
  - In this study, the preponderance of respondents in monogamous relationships and the expressed desire of single gay men to create monogamous relationships suggests a sweeping shift toward greater monogamy in younger gay men.

- A small, but significant number of couples described themselves as monogamous, even though they had 'three-ways' and/or occasional sex with 'outsiders.' We described these couples as 'monogamish' and had them self-identify in the qualitative survey.

- Marriage is definitely becoming the norm.
  - In our quantitative study, 15% of couples are married; 26% are domestic partners; 36% are intending to marry. A whopping 92% of single men expect to marry. 62% said most of their friends are married or likely to marry.
  - Marriage was equally prevalent among monogamous and non-monogamous couples.
  - Monogamy was equated with marriage by 58% of all respondents. However 31% viewed non-monogamy as an option for a married couple with 11% being unsure.

- Despite the myths and the anecdotal horror stories, both monogamous and non-monogamous couples can have enduring, healthy and happy relationships.

- Contrary to the fears and myths, long-term couples (both monogamous and non-monogamous) most frequently have enduring, satisfying sex lives within their primary relationships.

- We identified respondents by ethnicity and had good representation of major groupings in the US. We did not find significant differences corresponding to ethnicity.

Chapter 2
Overall Study Results

Inclination toward Monogamy

Probably the most striking finding of this study is that younger gay men seem to be more inclined toward monogamy than their elders. In our current study, both the preponderance of respondents in monogamous relationships and the expressed desire of single gay men to create a monogamous relationship seems to represent a sweeping shift toward greater monogamy.

In the quantitative study, most of the 580 participants came via FaceBook:

- 42% of respondents were single
- 50% of our respondents were in monogamous relationships
- 8% of our respondents were in non-monogamous relationships

Of the couples, 86% were monogamous and 14% were non-monogamous. Of the single respondents, 90% stated they were seeking monogamous relationships. Even in our Grindr cohort (which we would assume is skewed toward non-monogamy) 81% of the 325 singles were seeking monogamy.

Research conducted previously characterizes almost half of long-term (3+ years) gay relationships as non-monogamous (Shernoff, LCSW, 2007). In 2010 researchers at San Francisco State University carried out a study that revealed just how common open relationships are among partnered gay men and lesbians in the Bay Area. As *The New York Times* reported: "The Gay Couples Study... fol-lowed 556 male couples for three years – about 50 percent of those surveyed have sex outside their relationships, with the knowledge and approval of their partners." That figure is similar to another survey done by CHEST (Dr. Jeffrey T. Parsons, director of Hunter College's Center for HIV Educational Studies and Training) which found 58% gay male couples identified as monogamous and 42% as non-monogamous.

Amongst younger gay men, there is a smaller, but still substantive group inclined toward non-monogamy.

- 14% of our respondents who were in couples, were in committed non-monogamous relationships.
- 12% of respondents' previous relationships had been non-monogamous and an additional 15% of respondents stated they had had both monogamous and non-monogamous relationships previously. Thus, 27% of respondents had some experience of being in a non-monogamous relationship.

While the large majority are inclined toward monogamy, there is also a group in the middle that is open to the possibility of non-monogamy under the right circumstances.

- Of our single respondents, 34% stated they could imagine agreeing to a non-monogamous relationship with the right person and 32% stated they might consider opening a relationship and having it become non-monogamous depending on the length of the relationship.

○ In our Grindr cohort (which we would assume is skewed toward non-monogamy) the numbers were a bit higher: 51% of single men were open to non-monogamy with the right person; 52% can imagine opening the relationship over time.

○ We hypothesize that some couples will move to non-monogamy over time. We refer to our previous study (*Beyond Monogamy*, Spears, Lowen, 2010.) as a point of reference. In that study, which solely looked at long-term non-monogamous couples, 49% began their relationships being non-monogamous, but the other 51% were still monogamous after 1 year. It took the 51% from 1 year to 26 years to open their relationship (the average time being 6.6 years).

Age as factor in inclination toward monogamy:

On the one hand, the preference for monogamy seemed to cut across ages.

Singles 25 & under: 89% were seeking monogamous relationships.

Singles 26-30: 93% were seeking monogamous relationships.

Singles 31-40: 92% were seeking monogamous relationships

However, older respondents were more open to the possibility of a non-monogamous relationship.

44% of singles from 26-40 were open to the possibility.

29% of those 25 and under were open to the possibility.

Predictably, there were more non-monogamous couples in the older age groups

Of those, 25 & under: 4% were in non-monogamous relationships.

Of those, 26-30: 8% were in non-monogamous relationships.

Of those, 31-40: 11% were in non-monogamous relationships.

Additional Research Conducted in Prior Years on Non-monogamy in Male Couples

- Most research shows that approximately half to two-thirds of long-term male couples who have been together for five years or more are honestly non-monogamous (Shernoff, LCSW, 2007).

- The prevalence of non-monogamy in gay male relationships became widely known as the result of the ground-breaking book, *The Male Couple*, David McWhirter, M.D. and Andre Mattison, PhD., 1984. Based on interviews of 156 long-term couples, they found that after 5 years, all of the couples had incorporated some provision for outside sexual activity.

- Since the AIDS pandemic, four studies have found that gay men have not become more monogamous out of fear of HIV (Crawford, Rodden, Kippax & Van de Ven, 2001; Davidovich, et al., 2001; Halkitis, Zade, Shrem & Marmor, 2004; LaSala, 2005). Other studies document that only one third of male couples are sexually exclusive (*Advocate Sex Poll*, 2002; Bryant & Demian, 1994; LaSala, 2004; Wagner, Remien & Carballo-Dieguez, 2000).

- One study contradicts these. In that study, 70% of men in male couples reported being monogamous and viewed any outside sex as betrayal of commitment (Campbell, 2000).

Is the shift toward monogamy perceived as generational?

In this study, the large percentages of monogamous relationships and the fact that 90% of the single men were seeking a monogamous relationship, certainly would lead one to assume there's a generational shift. Our questions directed toward the generational shifts support this, but it is not as clear cut as we might assume.

Only 25% of respondents agreed with the statement, "My generation tends to be more monogamous than preceding generations." This indicates some shift, but far from sweeping. Likewise, a majority, but not an overwhelming majority, of single respondents and respondents in monogamous relationships agreed with the statement, "The couples I know that are near my age consider themselves monogamous (57% and 69% respectively).

Percentage of respondents who agree with the following statements:	Single men	Monogamous	Non-Monogamous	Total
My generation tends to be more monogamous than preceding generations	22%	29%	19%	25%
The couples I know that are near my age consider themselves monogamous	57%	69%	42%	60%

The comments in the qualitative study and in the interviews reflected a shift, but again it wasn't sweeping. The majority of comments indicated monogamy was becoming the norm:

"I think that younger men are more oriented toward monogamy. There's more assimilation and with that comes more embracement of the mainstream ideal. Monogamy, marriage, having children – it's all more attainable than in the past."

"The majority of my friends want monogamy. I think it's because we grew up in a more open society. Sex wasn't ever furtive and we didn't have to get what we could when it was available. From what I've heard, there were hidden clubs, colored handkerchiefs, and ways of letting someone know you're available. We can be open about it without getting beat up. We don't have to get what we can while we can. Some of my younger friends aren't monogamous, but they're still sowing their oats. When they're done with Grindr, they will probably want a long-term relationship."

"Race and religion have had no bearing, but community has. My friends are in monogamous relationships and I think that influences us."

Whereas previous generations tended to think of monogamy or non-monogamy in absolute, 'all or nothing' terms, some respondents commented that the younger generations espouse monogamy, but hold it a bit more loosely:

"Most guys that are single are looking for monogamy. They're not any different than straight people. I think monogamy is assumed. Non-monogamy is a mode you have to actively decide upon. It's threatening. I had a friend from college tell me that non-monogamy is a sign a relationship is failing – that it's not a real relationship, but I think younger people (gay and straight) are more relaxed and loose around the edges. The topic of 'monogamish' doesn't really come up but I have friends who have been in situations when they would pick up someone, but they consider it an outlier – they're still monogamous in their minds. The lines are more blurred; relationships evolve. You see characters on TV who are non-monogamous, so you know it's an option."

"My friends and I agree to be monogamous – I'd say 80% of us. But a lot of them end up being non-monogamous. They open their relationship over time and set up rules, although it doesn't always work out."

"With our friends we do talk about it and it's pretty split. We kid the monogamous couples and they kid us. There's not judgment. My guess is there may be more monogamy with younger men who are less experienced sexually. Perhaps if they're newly coming out or are out in fairly non-gay areas of the country where monogamy is more the norm. We definitely see a trend toward 'monogamish.' A lot of couples don't want the label of being non-monogamous. We know a few couples who have three-ways, but they consider themselves monogamous."

"Among our peers, they tend to have relationships that are monogamous. However, I see a lot of long-term gay relationships that are 'monogamish.' It's very sex positive that they can fool around and it won't threaten their relationship."

And some respondents reported their friends and their generations were still embracing non-monogamy:

"I have friends all over the spectrum. Gays tend to be non-monogamous; the straights identify as polyamorous. My best friend is monogamous. He tried to do an open relationship, but he got very jealous. I said, 'Hey, you tried, it's not right for you. He kids me about all my boyfriends.'"

"We have a good sized circle of friends – people in their 30's, 40's and even 50's. They are all pretty much non-monogamous, although to differing degrees. Some are non-monogamous, a few are polyamorous, and a few are swingers (straights). There isn't any judgment or weirdness between them. We do live in a predominantly Mormon community and so we're all supportive of each other's differences. I don't think it varies by their age and I doubt any of them consider themselves monogamous."

"I have a lot of older couple friends (mid-30s to late 40's) and they tend to have more sexually open relationships. However, our friends who are our age tend to be monogamous."

"I think that it's not shifting toward monogamy, but couples are more secretive about being open because it's taboo, and different from their families who were monogamous. I think that the generation after mine might be more open about being less monogamous. I find that when I talk with them they are often monogamish."

"I don't know a single gay monogamous couple in DC, but in Memphis everyone was monogamous. I think it depends partly on the size of the town and the norms around you."

"All of my young friends want to get married and the 'white picket fence', but they get disenchanted with it, as it's not what they expect it to be and they become bitter. We have some other friends who are also non-monogamous, like us. There are also some who are legitimately monogamous. However, a lot of them are 'monogamish' couples, some of whom are actually just cheating."

"We hang out with people from our ages (27, partner is 40) to 40' – 50's. They're all pretty much non-monogamous; they all have different degrees of monogamy than others. I don't think that any of the couples consider themselves as monogamous."

"I feel like my generation's problems with monogamy are that they're too quick to give up. In the best relationships I've had, I simply had no interest in anyone but the one I was dating. On the other hand, I have friends who enter a new relationship and seem to never delete their Grindr accounts, so they just continue to get bombarded by opportunity. It seems like they then jump to an open relationship to address their fear of missing out."

Those who observed a generational shift toward monogamy had various hypotheses as to why. The most common explanation was the acceptance of gays and their integration into the mainstream culture. A corresponding theory was that older gay men had developed much more promiscuous norms because of the furtiveness of sex and the way gay liberation had been defined and had evolved.

"With gays getting more integrated, we no longer have to hide who we are. Having a monogamous relationship seems more available/possible."

"The younger generation is finding a lot more people being accepting and our rights are growing. As we become more accepted, gays are having children and forming beautiful bonds with each other. Before, a lot of gays were married to women and cheating, but that isn't the case now. It makes sense that people would become more monogamous now."

"Older gay men may not be as serious about monogamy since they had to lead secret lives and are trying to play catch up. You do that for a while and then it becomes the norm. With more acceptance, there's more freedom to be normal."

"The majority of our friends in relationships are in monogamous relationships, but I also know a number of non-monogamous couples. I theorize that perhaps the trend toward monogamy might be that what's being pushed in society. We now have the right to marry and some feel that monogamy is part of that. It's hard to live an alternative lifestyle when you're trying to go mainstream."

"We're polyamorous, but our friends who are younger seem to be more idealistic with respect to monogamy. I think that there's a 'hetero-normative' energy among the younger generation now that marriage is a possibility and it's shaping their reactions.... These younger guys have grown up with the possibility of marriage and therefore some of that is associated with monogamy."

"My impression is that younger people are oriented more toward monogamy. The reason is the fact that gay culture is becoming assimilated into the mainstream, and monogamy is part of the assimilation. The idea of finding and settling down with your soul mate is desirable, and the fact that with gay marriage, that's more attainable now."

For us as study authors, who are members of the older generation and have spent 40 years together in an open relationship, these theories resonate. We recently saw The Normal Heart and it reminded us how directly sex was linked to the gay male identity and to gay liberation. When AIDS emerged, there was a huge resistance to pulling back from promiscuous and anonymous sex. The closing of the Baths was considered a betrayal of the gay community. We remember thinking that having gay sex was a political act and the more sex we had, the more liberated we felt. To be a long-term couple at that time, was to be an outlier. As gay men began to couple more, non-monogamy certainly fit the ethos of the era, more than monogamy.

How things will evolve, relative to relational norms, as gays are increasingly integrated into the mainstream is a fascinating source of conjecture. Where acceptance of the declared societal dictate of monogamy fits into the gay culture vs. "gays defining our relationships in our own terms" will be one of the bellwethers of what that integration portends.

Support for Monogamy and Non-monogamy

Interestingly, we heard from both monogamous and non-monogamous camps that there is a lack of support. On the one hand, those in monogamous relationships felt like there was a history of promiscuity in the gay community and that non-monogamy was considered the norm. They found a lack of respect for their desire to be exclusive.

"I don't feel supported by the gay community in having a monogamous relationship. In fact, the norm seems to be open relationships, and we feel judged, and even pressured, to open things up, when people find out we're monogamous."

"I feel as if non-monogamous relationships are something that are expected of gay men, an idea that we are incapable of forming a single family unit. Homosexual or heterosexual, we all have desires and attractions directed towards people that we are not in a relationship with. However implying that we cannot control and or are not capable of maintaining a monogamous relationship takes away from us as a people. I believe the role of a monogamous relationship in the gay community shows the evolution of our place in society. Before, I felt as if I was undeserving of that or simply unfit for it because I was gay, and that's not true."

On the other side of the coin, some non-monogamous couples felt monogamy was expected, not just from straight people, but also within the gay community. As gays become more integrated into the larger society and gay marriage becomes common, they questioned if there wasn't a tendency to 'mimic' straight relationships.

"Trying to explain our relationship status to other people can be challenging. Friends and family members who have more traditional views of romance and commitment are often confused."

"We have encountered some disapproval from other gay men regarding our behavior, but this hasn't caused any trouble for our relationship. Some gay men are much more attached to emulating traditional sexual norms (and gender roles), so we realize we have to be more guarded around certain friends."

"There is too much 'slut shaming' among single gay men towards non-monogamous gay men. I feel like we have to be in the closet or we'll be judged as if we were a gay couple justifying our relationship to straights. Why these single and some coupled men think their relationship must look like a 60s' family TV show is beyond me. I think their rigidity is why many of them are still single and or unhappily coupled. When everything has to live up to an unrealistic paradigm, things have a tendency to fall apart."

Is there something between Monogamy and Non-monogamy?

"Do spontaneous threesomes with your partner mean you're not monogamous?"

"I feel there should be an option on the survey for having done a threesome once. I consider our relationship monogamous despite us having a threesome once because I consider a non-monogamous relationship to be one where sex with another outside the relationship occurs more often. I felt there was no way for me to clearly answer the monogamy question."

"I wish the survey had given options on agreed sexual encounters outside the relationship where both partners participate. I don't see that as non-monogamous or open. It's not so black and white. I know of couples who consider themselves monogamous and closed that occasionally have sexual liaisons outside the relationship together as a couple."

"I think there are so many more levels of monogamy that it can't be separated into two categories. There are a lot of agreements that can happen between couples that they consider monogamous that could fall in a grey area."

As we mentioned in the Methodology segment, when analyzing the Facebook and Grindr quantitative data, we noticed there were a significant number of couples who described themselves as monogamous, but acknowledged in the open comment box that they had 'three-ways' and/or occasional sex with 'outsiders.'

In the previously mentioned CHEST study, couples identified themselves as monogamous, monogamish or open. CHEST explains on its website: "Typically gay men have been categorized as monogamous or not, and our data show that it is not so black and white."

The CHEST survey indicated that about 60% of respondents were single and 40% were partnered. Of those partnered, about 58% were in monogamous relationships. Of those that were non-monogamous, 53% were in open relationships, and 47% were in "monogamish" relationships (i.e., couples that have sex with others as a couple such as "three-ways" or group sex).

We were curious about this, and when we conducted our qualitative survey, we had respondents identify as Monogamous, Non-monogamous, or Monogamous, but held 'loosely' — 'Monogamish.' Out of 853 respondents, 20% categorized themselves as 'loosely monogamous' with 45 of these completing written comments.

"We consider ourselves monogamous, but we're still figuring out what that means to us. We've had the occasional threesome, but that doesn't feel like non-monogamous activity since we're participating together. I think there are various ways to be monogamous and various spectrums of openness that need to be defined and discussed more."

"It is really important that people understand that there are many forms of non-monogamy. Relationships are not simply open or closed. The experiences of 'monogamish,' swingers, fully open relationships, and polyamorous people are all very different from each other, and lumping them all together like this really doesn't help the surveyors to understand what it is to be non-monogamous."

Because this seems to be a significant trend, we have devoted an entire section to responses from 'monogamish' couples about what they do and how they view their relationship. *See page 49.*

Marriage is increasingly becoming the norm

LBGT marriage is prevalent and it's safe to say is increasingly becoming the norm. It clearly is embraced by non-monogamous couples as much as it is by monogamous couples:

Percentage of respondents who agree with the following statements:	Single men	Monogamous	Non-Monogamous	Total
Most of the long-term couples I know are married or likely to become married	57%	75%	68%	64%

Does Marriage imply monogamy?

When asked whether they agree with the statement, "In my mind, gay marriage implies monogamy," 80% of monogamous couples agreed marriage implied monogamy. This is a marked difference from non-monogamous couples where only 26% equated the two.

Percentage of respondents who agree with the following statements:	Single men	Monogamous	Non-Monogamous	Total
In my mind, gay marriage implies monogamy	65%	80%	26%	65%

"As far as commitment, marriage and monogamy are the same. On the other hand, it's perfectly normal and acceptable to try new things with your partner so I guess you could be married without being monogamous. I see marriage giving our relationship that extra oomph of trust."

"For us, I think we equate marriage with monogamy, but we have friends who are married and have been together 13 years and they're non-monogamous. We're married, but we may still consider opening up the relationship down the road."

"We're monogamous, but based on my experience, monogamy and marriage don't necessarily go together. A lot of guys happen to be more promiscuous and forthright with their sexual desires."

Of course, some respondents saw marriage completely distinct from monogamy.

"I do not think that monogamy is required because you are married. If two responsible adults can communicate their desires then I see no reason that it cannot still work out."

"Marriage doesn't necessarily imply monogamy. Your relationship should be however you and your husband want it to be."

"We're married and non-monogamous and we definitely don't equate marriage with monogamy."

"We just recently married. I don't see marriage and monogamy as one and the same. Marriage is a commitment to a person and the terms you created are up to the two people making that commitment. As long as you are on the same page, that's what should matter. Are you committing to your partner becoming primary in your life?"

Relationship Health

"We're not infatuated 100% of the time. In the long run, it's really about developing a strong partnership. The Cinderella fantasy doesn't last forever — ultimately it becomes about friendship, kinship, partnership — that's what's most important."

This statement could have been offered from either monogamous or non-monogamous couples. Both monogamous and non-monogamous couples characterized their relationships as healthy and spoke of the important qualities of partnership.

In the two most pertinent questions about relationship health, there was no difference between monogamous and non-monogamous couples. Both monogamous and non-monogamous couples viewed themselves as having a healthy, stable relationship and described that relationship as one they found satisfying.

Percentage of respondents who agree with the following statements:	Monogamous	Non-Monogamous
"We have a healthy, stable relationship."	93%	93%
"Our relationship makes me happy/satisfied."	94%	91%

On three other questions that might correlate with relationship health, responses from both monogamous and non-monogamous participants were again affirmative. The three questions related to fighting fairly, behaving honestly and the expectation that the relationship would last. On these three questions, there were only minor differences between monogamous and non-monogamous respondents.

Correlates to Relationship Health

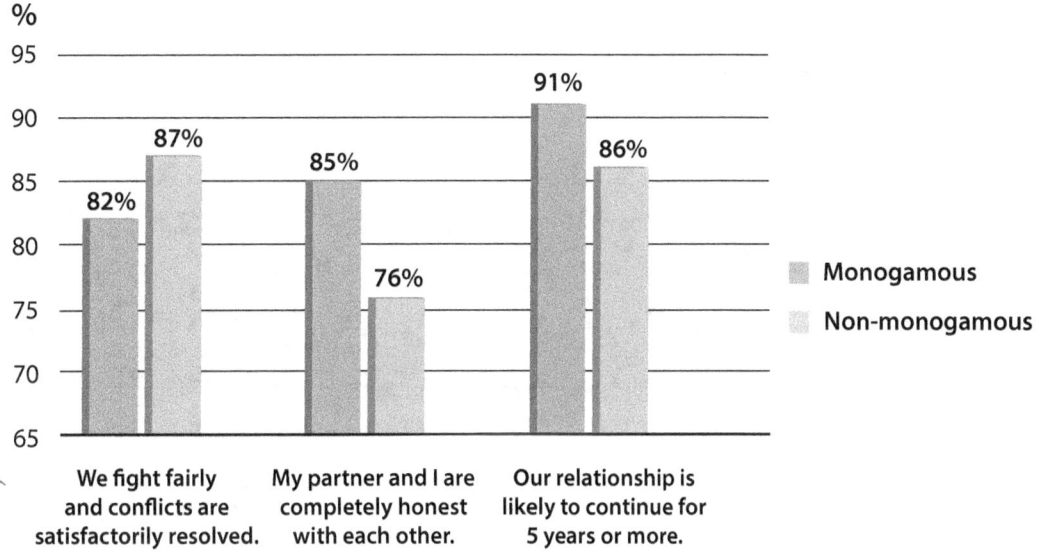

The degree of honesty had the largest variance. Non-monogamous partners reported that 76% thought their partner and they were completely honest with each other. This is lower than the 85% of monogamous couples who felt this way. Correspondingly, of the non-monogamous couples, 5% strongly disagreed with the statement about honesty and 2% of monogamous strongly disagreed. Although our numbers aren't different enough to claim statistical significance, it is an intriguing difference nonetheless. A contributing factor may be the 'don't ask, don't tell' policy of some non-monogamous couples.

Although not fully predictive, the longevity of a relationship correlates with relationship health. Respondents clearly expected their relationships to last. However, the length of time couples had been together in this study was relatively short. The average length being 3.2 years, with 29% still in the first year of their relationship. This is markedly shorter than our previous study with non-monogamous couples where the minimum length of time in relationship was 8 years (required for study participation) and the average relationship length was 16 years. We don't consider the length of the relationships in this study long enough to suggest any correlation with relationship health.

Sex Lives Together & Apart

The results on the questions asking about sex lives certainly puts to rest the notion that long-term couples can't continue a healthy sex life together. Contrary to the fears and myths, long-term couples (both monogamous and non-monogamous) most frequently have enduring, satisfying sex lives within their primary relationships. 83% of the monogamous respondents were satisfied with their sex lives together. Non-monogamous responses were somewhat less, with 71% claiming to be satisfied with their sex lives together.

	Monogamous	Non-Monogamous
Our sex life with each other is satisfying	83%	71%

Frequency of Sex with Partner

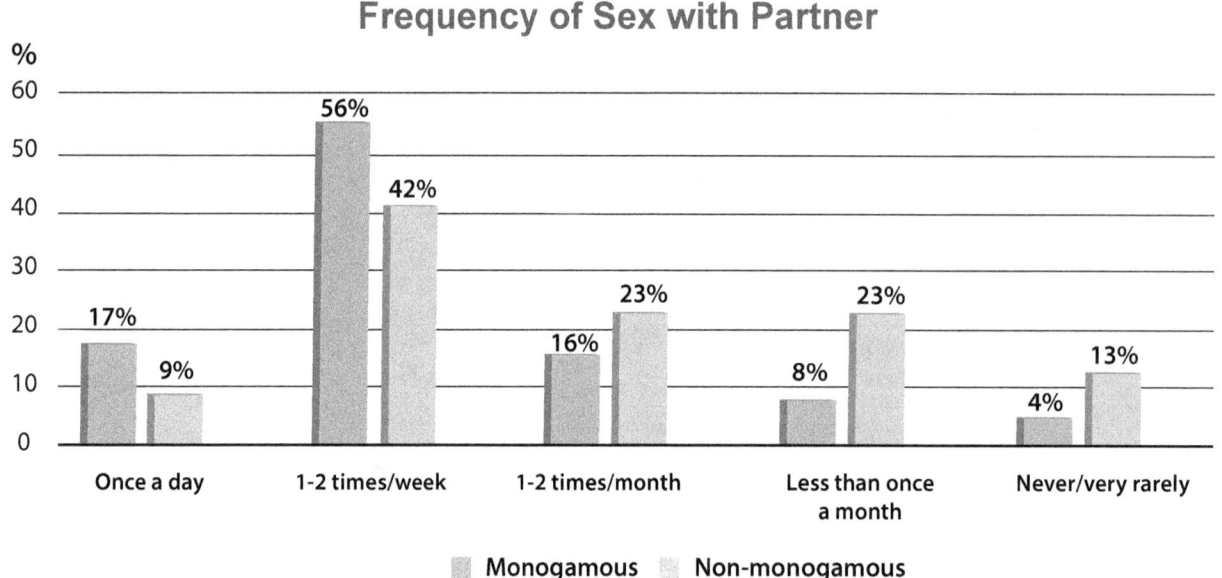

	Monogamous	Non-monogamous
Once a day	17%	9%
1-2 times/week	56%	42%
1-2 times/month	16%	23%
Less than once a month	8%	23%
Never/very rarely	4%	13%

Frequency of sex varied with monogamous respondents having somewhat more frequent sex with their partners. 73% of monogamous and 51% of non-monogamous respondents had sex with their partners at least 1-2 times per week. 12% of monogamous respondents and 36% of non-monogamous respondents stated they have sex together less than once a month.

Both monogamous and non-monogamous respondents spoke about continuing to experiment, build in fantasy, and spice things up as a way of tending to their sex lives together. The desire for couples to keep their sex lives active and satisfying as their relationship progresses over the years is discussed in greater depth in the sections following on monogamous and non-monogamous relationships.

Chapter 3
Monogamous Relationships

PERSONAL PROFILE #1
Tory and Sam

Tory is 25 years old and Sam is 34. They got together when Tory
was 16 years old and have been together for 9 years.

"We got engaged a month ago and as of this morning; in Texas we can get married."

"I grew up in a Pentecostal Christian family with no music or dancing. I felt betrayed by religion, but I'm still spiritual. I think being monogamous stems from the positive underlying ideals that shaped me."

"We've been monogamous since the beginning. It's working pretty well. There are ups and downs, but I absolutely wouldn't change it. As we get older and establish ourselves, we are increasingly happy and content being together. I think it's helped our relationship last."

"4 or 5 years into the relationship, during one of our down periods, sex felt stagnant — it felt old. I began questioning. 'How do I know this is the right man? I'm still young. I haven't had many experiences. What am I missing?' Sam and I talked about it. He got mad, but we're fine now. Sex re-elevated itself — I think because we became more content."

"The majority of my friends are monogamous. A few friends aren't, but I don't have any judgments about that. I'm not into pushing what's right for me onto others. I do think my generation is more monogamous. When I read about earlier eras, I don't think I would have handled it all that well. Coming out was hard enough, I'm glad I came out when the environment was more supportive. I think when it used to be harder, being gay got suppressed and could only come out in sex. Maybe that's why there was more emphasis on multiple partners. I know for me, I'm more comfortable being with one person."

Choosing Monogamy

Our study results and interviews suggest that most couples came to the agreement to be monogamous without too much difficulty. 88% of our 290 monogamous respondents said both they, and their partner, preferred having a monogamous relationship. In our previous research, we found more angst, need for discussion, and sometimes conflict when couples decided to be non-monogamous.

While most couples expressed a strong desire for monogamy, the majority did not hold negative judgments about non monogamy or non monogamous couples. In fact, many held an open mind about the potential of their relationship evolving to include 'outsiders' in some fashion. Usually, this was a stance against 'certainty' — "never, say never". But some held opening their relationship as a real possibility, although it wasn't what they wanted currently.

On the other side of the coin, 14% of monogamous respondents reported having arguments about opening their relationship and a few stated they would prefer non-monogamy, but were comfortable with doing what their partner wanted.

9% shared they might break up because of issues related to monogamy. We would assume this fits with the 12% of couples where both don't prefer monogamy. However, it could also additionally be related to the 25% who acknowledged having outside sex without prior agreement.

Reasons for being Monogamous

In our qualitative survey, we asked respondents about their reasons for being monogamous. We had 161 responses with many participants listing several reasons.

Reasons for being Monogamous	Percent Identifying Reason (N=161)
Love	26%
No need for more: Devoted to each other	21%
It's what we believe in	19%
No STD's	14%
Commitment	13%
Jealousy; Could cause problems	12%
Respect and consideration for my partner	11%
Trust	11%
Closer; Build a stronger bond	9%
Wouldn't be comfortable being with another; wouldn't be comfortable sharing him	8%
Our sex is special; It gives us an exclusive status; Greater intimacy	5%
BF wants it	3%

We grouped comments by theme with the following being the predominant reasons:

Theme	Reasons for being Monogamous	Percent Identifying Theme/comment (N=161)
Emotional Commitment		
	Love	26%
	No need for more: Devoted to each other	21%
	Commitment	13%
	Our sex is special; It gives us an exclusive status; Greater intimacy	5%
Creates a Strong Foundation		
	Respect and consideration for my partner	11%
	Trust	11%
	Closer; Build a stronger bond	9%
What we Believe In		
	It's what we believe in	19%
The Pragmatic		
	No STD's	14%
	Jealousy; Could cause problems	12%
	Wouldn't be comfortable being with another; wouldn't be comfortable sharing him	8%
	BF wants it	3%

Emotional Commitment

There were several reasons to the theme of emotional commitment. Not surprisingly, 'love' was at the top of the list. Not much was written about 'love', but it was on 41 participant's lists (26%).

"Love is special and treasured. Having one person in your life that you connect with and share everything with is what makes Love LOVE."

"My partner and I are best friends, and we are meant to be together. We have been together for almost 8 years, and we love being together. We love each other's families, and we have a great life. We want to grow old together, and we want to share our lives together. I cannot imagine being with anyone else, and neither can he."

Closely related was the desire to focus and depend solely on one other person (21%) and to make a commitment to that one person (13%)

When I met my partner, I didn't look at anyone like I looked at him. He grabbed my full attention. I also felt comfortable to be myself and safe around him. So I didn't need anything from anyone else."

"We do not see any reason to bring someone else into our relationship. We are happy with each other. We enjoy each other's company and want to give our love to only one person."

"Love is not lust and infatuation through the entirety of the relationship. Love is compromise, but more importantly partnership. I don't see the need to sacrifice what I've spent 5 years of my life building, to throw it away on a casual hook-up. If I wanted to fuck around, I'd be single; I don't wish to fuck around."

"He's the only one who was as emotionally invested in me as physically, and once I found that, I knew what I had was special - I don't need anything else."

Most saw sex being an expression of their love and 5% mentioned that their sexual exclusivity was a reward and/or a pathway to greater intimacy and meaning.

"I believe there is something sacred about sex when it's kept between two people who care for each other. There's an element that can't be felt through casual sex and random partners."

"Being monogamous gives our sexual relationship an exclusive status - which means it is more meaningful, or special."

"Sex within a relationship has a deeper, more worthwhile meaning, because we love each other and the ultimate sign of love is monogamy."

Creates a strong foundation for the relationship

9% spoke of monogamy encouraging closeness and creating stronger bonds and 11% commented that monogamy and commitment provided a safety net of trust.

"We feel like monogamy is necessary to keep a relationship intimate and reach the levels of trust and communication needed for a fulfilling and meaningful bond with one another."

"Right now, we feel monogamy is best for us. We have been together for 9 months and our bond grows stronger every day. Currently, there is no need nor is there room in our growing bond for the sexual experience of another."

"We believe that being monogamous in a relationship sets the foundation for us to build a life together. We feel that if you cannot be monogamous then you should be single, where you can do what you want without hurting anyone else."

"We are firm believers that the best way you can respect your partner is to give yourself fully to them. Some people have "needs" that make monogamy impossible for them, but our love outweighs any sexual desire we might have. We are certainly open and understand that our bond may evolve, but the feeling of being equals is important to us."

11%, viewed monogamy as the best way to respect and honor their partner. Monogamy was a way of being considerate of their partner's feelings.

"Monogamy lends itself to consideration of each other's feelings and mutual respect."

"I love my partner a lot and would not do anything that would hurt him and I believe that not being monogamous would hurt him deeply."

"It's a way of having respect for my partner and being respectful of his insecurities."

It's what we believe in

For 19%, monogamy is what they believed in. For some, this stemmed from beliefs about love and their definition of a healthy relationship.

"Being in a relationship is between you and the person you are in love with. That's the way it's supposed to be."

"We are monogamous because we respect what a relationship should be about. It is not about sex or physical standards. It is about love and maintaining a relationship with someone you care about and trust. The 'hook-up culture' is a real issue and it is embarrassing. It is lessening the value of sexual relations and it is making it harder for people to become committed."

"I'm Catholic and we're pretty strict about relationships. Once you're married, you're married and monogamy is expected. Believing that has helped me with monogamy. The downside is I can feel trapped."

"We believe that monogamy is the fullest, most complete way of expressing our love for and commitment to one another. We also have spiritual reasons for espousing monogamy."

"I'm very traditional, and I believe there can only be one person for you, It's a matter of respect and trust. Besides the gay community is very promiscuous - you sleep with one, you've slept with them all."

"I feel like true love isn't something that is shared with someone else. When you truly love someone, then you are not going to look at your partner as someone whose body is just for fun. It's something that's intimate between the two of you, so you have to respect each other even when times are hard. Random sex isn't what's going to make you last, but a true love and a bit of selfishness of keeping what's yours will."

"Being with someone you love shouldn't be about who your next fuck will be. We're monogamous because we love each other – being with that one person that makes you feel like you're flying every time you kiss. Sex is something that you share with the person you love. Being able to get close to someone to have them know your weaknesses and your fears. I've never really liked the whole, 'I'm gay and let's fuck this one and that one.' It makes no sense to me."

"My partner and I both feel monogamy works for us. We have no interest in seeing other people."

"Today we have no need to hide our sexuality and therefore can integrate ourselves into the monogamous normative belief-system which promotes healthy and fulfilling spiritual bonds. Non-monogamy does not promote spiritual growth because it solely promotes physical lust and selfishness. If a person is to discover their true selves untainted by the physical sexual urges, monogamy is a key ingredient."

For some, it wasn't so much a belief as it was a function of what they had experienced in their lives. Monogamy was rooted in traditional values, having observed it working for their parents, and wanting to be close and accepted by family. It was assumed, without much consideration.

"It was an automatic assumption – we have a traditional mindset and this is the deep South. It makes sense to devote your time and attention to one person. Non-monogamy would feel like we're being unfaithful to each other even if it was a three-way. It would create instability. It would mean the relationship was flawed and we weren't enough together."

"I was raised Lutheran – that shaped me somewhat, although I'm atheist now. Regardless, my values are around stability, growing old together, raising a family. I'm planning on having kids. We have the option of marriage and pursuing a family."

PERSONAL PROFILE #2
Steven and Luis

Steven, 30, and Luis, 24 have been together 5 years.

"Our parents were monogamous and we have their values. We both were in agreement about wanting to be monogamous. We discussed experiences with friends who were in open relationships and knew we didn't want that. In one situation, we saw them experiencing a high level of jealousy and it was hard for them to resolve that issue. We also couldn't imagine having someone we hardly know coming into our home."

"Being monogamous helps the relationship be healthy. Being consistent allows us to be closer. We don't have any conflict to worry about. We're both close with our families and that's easier without anyone else involved. Our straight friends see us as dependable and reliable. We're both from Catholic backgrounds. We're not religious per se, but our upbringing and the experience with our families has shaped our values. My parents were married 50 years and his 35 years and our siblings are all monogamous. Everyone – my parents, aunts and uncles have stayed together, even after tough times."

"When we met, Luis was here illegally. He had to be deported to make it legal. We were separated for a year without sex. We both got very jealous of each other's friends at the time even though neither of us were cheating. We talked about it. We needed extra reassurance. It was hard being separated - we didn't know if he would be able to come back."

"When Luis was younger he was sexually abused and so he's somewhat restrained around sex. When I discovered that (in our second year) I was able to be more understanding of his approach to sex. At that point, I shared with him that I had been totally into pornography and even though I had given it up, I had a higher engagement in sex because of my pornography. He was accepting and it helped to understand why we were both the way we were. We got closer and trusted each other more."

"What we've learned is there will be desires and other people involved in our lives that are tempting. Communication is the most critical thing. We agree on the same moral values and we stay true. It's okay for others to not be monogamous, but we want to stay monogamous."

The Pragmatic

The rest of the reasons could loosely be grouped as 'pragmatic.' For 14%, the primary reason for being monogamous was related to health risk. Others mentioned this as an added benefit.

> *"I feel monogamy is the safest way to prevent sexually transmitted diseases. With each new partner, before the condom comes off, we each get tested – this way we both feel good about being clean and don't have to worry. Also I make it known from the start that I'm more willing to forgive them if they cheat as long as they inform me before we have sex again. This is because to me that shows they care enough to protect my body from diseases than trying to hide the fact that they were unfaithful."*

For 12%, monogamy was preferred out of a desire to avoid problems they associated with non-monogamy. For some, it was the fear of jealousy; for others, it was not wanting the complications or the relationship risks that non-monogamy introduces.

> *"We trust each other very much but feel that introducing external sex partners would complicate our relationship and introduce some jealousy that is not necessary."*

> *"For us, the relationship is about my partner and me, and bringing another person in for either a three-way or allowing each other to be with others sexually would only cause problems. When we discussed the idea of monogamy we both agreed that we would not be able to be comfortable seeing the other with someone else. We see our relationship as not needing to be clouded by discomfort, and so choose not to be open. It just doesn't work for our psychologies."*

> *"Personally, I am the jealous type and have problems sharing. Plus, I was in a relationship once where we had threesomes and it backfired on me and opened up the door to cheating. All in all, I have a problem seeing the guy I'm with be in another man's arms, hold another man's hand, or even kiss another guy."*

> *"I don't think that one person can satisfy another person totally (sexually, emotionally and intellectually). You have to determine what is important to you (Is having a closed relationship and a family more important than having outside sex or other relationships?). I don't have a strong pull toward or against monogamy. Probably, my partner and I could be in a non-monogamous relationship. However, we are both jealous so it would be hard to do."*

Some spoke of the discomfort they would feel sharing their partner with another and some expressed a desire to know deeply that they are enough. (8%)

"We are both very selfish individuals and the idea of another person being with my partner makes me angry. It also makes me think that I am not enough."

"I would feel like he wanted to get it elsewhere because I wasn't pleasing him."

"Neither of us would be comfortable 'sharing' and neither of us wants to be with anyone else. I was previously in an open relationship and it was depressing and not fulfilling – not feeling like I was enough for somebody."

3% of participants were inclined toward being non-monogamous, but chose monogamy because of their partner's preference.

"It was non-negotiable. My partner is very much against open relationships. He calls himself an 'old school romantic.' He doesn't think you should want to be with anyone else when you're coupled. I would be open to having an occasional three-way if we met a friend and it clicked, but he's not open to anything other than strict monogamy. I'm happy with him and so I don't have any problem deciding to be monogamous."

"My partner thinks that being polyamorous is cheating in a certain way and that he would not like to share me with anyone else. I am strictly monogamous because he is not open to non-monogamy. I am choosing to have him over leading a polyamorous life."

"It's what he wants. I wanted to mess around together but he has had poor previous experiences with similar arrangements. We have several times, but now are completely monogamous."

Benefits of being Monogamous

In the quantitative survey, we asked about personal benefits in being monogamous. In many cases the benefits and reasons for being monogamous overlap. Out of 290 respondents, below are the percentages who agreed with the following statements:

Benefits of being Monogamous	Percentage
Encourages trust and security	68%
Encourages connection and closeness	63%
It feels right – it's the way it should be	62%
Makes us more likely to stay together	58%
Minimizes conflict and hurt feelings	52%
It prevents or minimizes jealousy and envy	48%
Encourages us to attend to the sex we have together	40%

We also asked about the benefits of being monogamous in the qualitative study, Answers correlated strongly with the quantitative responses about benefits. Below are the benefits coupled with representative comments from the qualitative survey and follow-up interviews.

Encourages trust and security—68%

The most commonly-named pay-off was trust and security. Comments about trust, loyalty, and the feeling of faithfulness were numerous.

"We can both trust each other completely! Neither of us has ever had to question the other's feelings towards us."

"The payoffs of monogamy? Being cared for; Never feeling alone; Someone to do things with; Never having to look for sex; Feeling secure and loved."

"A total commitment to monogamy has strengthened our overall commitment to one another; it has greatly reduced the potential for jealousy, and it has encouraged us to reply on each other. We couldn't believe that we are completely given to one another if we were not monogamous."

"The pay-off's are security and the comfort of having somebody there for me at the end of the day - no matter what. Not being under constant scrutiny gives me a greater sense of self."

"We assume that we wouldn't feel the same security and intimacy if we were non-monogamous."

Encourages connection and closeness—63%

Monogamy encourages connection and closeness. Comments referred to enhanced intimacy and the feeling of a deeper love.

> *"We are not close-minded to think monogamy is the only way, but we believe it has boosted our trust in each other and allows us to be on an equal level."*

> *"An intense love that only the two of us share. I cannot see myself with any other man. I love him and cannot wait to be married to this man."*

> *"It's easier to spoil one person with your love than multiple people. Take road trips, buy stupid little surprises, leave love notes. Inside jokes and finishing each-other's sentences will start to be unplanned and natural."*

> *"Monogamy is a way to tell your partner how much you love them and how much you care about them."*

> *"We both feel that we can share our deepest desires together without feeling judged at any point. Being open to different things and willing to share them with someone who means the world to you, makes the intimate relationship mean that much more."*

Makes us more likely to stay together—58%

58% said monogamy helps them stay together. The strong partnership that can flourish under monogamy was identified by many.

> *"We are growing together as one right now and monogamy is one of the ways we strengthen our bond. We are learning so much about ourselves and each other in many ways, including finances, spirituality, and politics."*

> *"We have created a home for ourselves – 2 dogs, a cat, and a turtle. We have put ourselves through school. We have our own apartment. I guess the payoff for being monogamous is knowing that we build each other up and motivate each other to do better. We have each other's best interest in mind and can completely put trust in each other without worry of the other's intentions being bad."*

> *"We have been able to live as a couple who help each other in whatever way when needed. We're unified financially and make the sacrifices necessary to take care of each other."*

"We have taught each other patience which is a big thing.... Things always work out, even if things get really bad. This is because we trust each other and because we love each other. Relationships are hard work, but in the end, when you find someone you love who loves you back with the same effort, it is so worth it."

"We have become each other's best friend. That is what is most important to us. We have amazing communication and intense amount of depth in our relationship, physically and emotionally."

"You can tend to your partner's needs and help develop and heal them. My partner came into my life after I had lost my grandma who I was extremely close with. One of the most beneficial things I have gotten from our monogamy is his full heart to help warm and heal mine."

"We have built a shared life together including buying a home and sharing a social circle. I have matured a lot in my relationship with my partner."

"The pay-off is a longer, healthier relationship – staying true to myself and another. We are fixing to get married and hopefully live the rest of our lives together."

Minimizes conflict, hurt feelings, jealousy and envy—52%

52% thought that monogamy minimizes the potential for jealousy, hurt feelings and the resulting conflict that come with them.

"No drama or jealousy about who is getting hit on more or who is getting more attention."

"I see less complications as a monogamous couple and more opportunities to focus on your partner."

"Knowing that the only person my partner is sexual with is me eases my mind about the stability of the relationship. There are no doubts or fears that someone might be able to provide sexual satisfaction that I cannot."

"I feel like I am enough. I feel wanted and desired and special - that I was chosen as the one person he would love."

Encourages us to attend to the sex we have together—40%

40% said monogamy helped their sex lives and made sex special.

> "We're able to be more open about what we want from one another sexually because we're not getting it elsewhere."

> "We are much more open to sexploration on our own, and pushing the limits to what we consider sexually appropriate, as we simply have to ask the other for something if we want it. Instead of either one of us saying "no" to something, and looking for it elsewhere, we discuss any sexual fantasy or need, and find a way to make that work creatively in our sexual relationship."

> "We are able to grow and experiment sexually and our sex is more meaningful because we're not sharing ourselves with anyone else."

> "One of the ways we communicate is through sex. Until we speak each other's love language fluently we have decided not to bring another into our bed."

Additional Benefits

Although not frequently stated, three distinct themes were identified in the qualitative responses that we had not included in the quantitative questions.

10 respondents mentioned Happiness and/or Joy:

> "The biggest payoff is true joy and happiness in our lives."

> "We get to spend a lot of time together and have learned to enjoy each other in every way. We have become more than lovers, we're best friends, and we love going out together."

> "I am able to recall "special moments" when the two of us are just alone being silly and downright obnoxious to each other. I feel like spreading that to more than one partner loses value and doesn't make the person feel like they are your world, when they are!"

> "I am the happiest I've ever been."

6 respondents spoke of becoming family and of family acceptance:

"It gives us a larger support system - both of our families are trusting and engaged in our relationship."

"My partner and I have become very close with each other. Out families have conversed and we are one big family and we are happy because of it."

"Because we're monogamous, I get to consistently see his hot dad and brother. Oh, and beefy cousin. And also his straight friends."

A final benefit mentioned by 5 people was "Others respect us":

"All of our friends and people in the gay community really respect us for it."

"Others respect us as an actual gay couple. They don't see us as sex-craved fools."

"It results in a large sense of normalcy and the respect of peers and family."

Challenges of being monogamous

In the quantitative survey, we asked about the challenges of being monogamous. Out of 290 respondents, here are the percentages who agreed with the following statements:

Theme	Challenges of being Monogamous for us Personally	Percentage
No Challenges		
	There are no real challenges to being monogamous	43%
Temptation		
	The desire for more variety in partners and types of sex	29%
	Staying faithful when I'd like to stray	18%
	Being honest about temptations and/or 'slip-ups'	18%
Jealousy		
	Jealousy/Envy even though outside sex is not involved	23%
Sex life is unsatisfying		
	Our sex life together is limited and/or un-satisfying	20%

There are no real challenges to being monogamous

43% agreed with the statement that they didn't find monogamy challenging. In the qualitative survey, where respondents were encouraged to identify challenges, only 8% of the 160 responded that there weren't any challenges. However, most of the challenges they identified, were framed in terms of success. Respondents acknowledged that at times, there are challenges, and spoke of what they found to be helpful. From the written comments and the interviews, we came away with the perspective that the vast majority did find monogamy required some work, but the benefits of monogamy were a strong motivator and reinforcement for that effort.

"Nothing is really challenging. We trust each other and want the same thing."

"To be honest there's not much we would consider challenging. We've never been in a fight since we talk through our problems, and we enjoy spending time together whenever we get the chance since we both have busy schedules."

"Nothing, really. Just don't rip his head off when you are fighting!"

"I don't think there is anything very challenging about monogamy. We trust each other, so we don't really have to worry about cheating. I don't find anything or anyone particularly tempting. I am in love and I guess that makes monogamy easy."

Temptation

For those who did acknowledge challenges, temptation was by far the most common struggle.

Statements related to Temptation	Percent Agreeing
The desire for more variety in partners and types of sex is a challenge.	29%
My partner or I have had sexual experiences outside our relationship without prior agreement	25%
Staying faithful when I'd like to stray is a challenge	18%
My partner or I have 'gotten involved' with someone else without prior agreement	18%
Being honest about temptations and/or 'slip-ups' is a challenge	18%

Below are comments from the qualitative survey and the interviews that are related to attractions and distractions – the desire for variety and the discipline of staying faithful.

"I find the urge to be with another person a challenge. After years of hook ups it's hard to stop wanting it. I handle it by thinking of my partner and how upset it would make him."

"From time to time, there is an urge to have sexual encounters with other men. Having the same thing over and over can get monotonous. My personal way of handling this is I watch porn. Sometimes, it will be for hours while my partner is at work and it all works up to an amazing ending and after that, I'm good!"

"The inability to just hook up with someone like I used to is challenging. I am a very flirty individual so when I go out with friends (without my partner) I am always chatting with people but know that I can't take it further than that even though a lot of times I really think about it."

"We really haven't been tempted to cheat. We find other guys attractive and talk openly about it. Even though we're monogamous, we have had 3-somes with other guys, but it's been rare. We do acknowledge that we jack off to porn."

"The most challenging part of being monogamous is not getting yourself in a position to cheat. If you know you're going to flirt when you're drunk around hot guys, don't get drunk around hot guys. If you're tempted by Grindr, don't log onto Grindr. Just avoid situations where you know you're likely to lapse rather than testing your willpower. Honestly, it's pretty easy."

"It's hard when I do see someone I want to sleep with but have to turn them down even when the offer is right in front of me. Trust and faithfulness are more important in the long run."

"The most challenging thing is how to handle a wandering eye and where is the line between 'inappropriate behavior' and 'conversation with other gay males'. We're all flirty beings and if two gay men find one another attractive it's very hard to tone down the lasciviousness. When I find myself in a position of being with another homosexual male whom I find attractive, I think of all of the things I'd lose in order to gain one lusty night with this stranger. Usually once I compare the two roads I could take, it immediately reaffirms my decision to stay with my boyfriend."

"Any time I see an attractive man at a club or bar, there is always a moment of slight temptation. Just because I am committed to my boyfriend doesn't mean I have gone blind to all the other men in the world. But as soon as my thoughts begin to wander, I remember my boyfriend and how much fun I have with him and how much I enjoy having sex with him, and I realize there isn't anything I would do to ruin that."

PERSONAL PROFILE #3
Terry and Tim

Terry is 38 and Tim is 41. They've been together 11 years.

"We were both raised conservatively. We never had a conversation, I just assumed we would be monogamous. During the first month, the condom broke and he said, "Well I have whatever you have now." And we didn't really look back. At Year 7, we talked about opening the relationship. We scheduled a three-way with a guy, who ended up getting gun-shy."

"When that didn't happen, we kept talking and decided we wanted to continue to be strictly monogamous. Since I was his first lover, my fear was he would find someone that is a much better lover than me. His fear was catching HIV or super-gonorrhea. I'm kind of glad it didn't happen. If he said he wanted to sleep with other people now, I'd probably be okay with it. Our relationship grows and changes - I never say 'Never.' He still adores me and brings me flowers. We got married three week ago and he said, "Thank you for choosing me 11 years ago." He still thinks I'm a prize. That's the greatest feeling in the world."

"After 11 years, you certainly notice other people. We say, "Just because you're on a diet doesn't mean you can't look at the menu." The first 5 years were like a honeymoon – sex 5 times a week. Around year 7, we went back to school and didn't have enough time together. That was really hard. Sex had slowed down. I asked friends if they had less sex and they reassured me it was normal. I was surprised and sad. I offered to split up and he said 'No.' We knew each other so well and he accepts me. We started working on the relationship and now it's wonderful. I want to feel needed and I get emotional and I need reassurance. He reassures me and then we're good. We still have date night. We're publically affectionate. Romance is important to me. Monogamy works, but you got to work at it."

"We have multigenerational friends. Half of our friends are non-monogamous. Two couples are in a foursome. They're deeply committed so does that mean they're monogamous? A lot of people are afraid to tell you they're not monogamous. I don't judge people so they often tell me."

"We both grew up pretty religious. Maybe we were just mimicking our parents. Our parents have been married 40+ years. Our families are very supportive of us. Now we're looking at adoption and having babies. We're working towards being able to afford children. For us, I think we equate marriage with monogamy, but we have friends who are married and have been together 13 years and their non-monogamous. We're married, but we may still consider opening up the relationship down the road."

"Temptation is natural at times, but when you have a Porsche, why fool around with a Toyota? A simple one night stand is not worth risking something unique and special that has been cultivated over time."

"Honestly, I find other guys attractive and I have a high-functioning libido. I handle it by understanding that there are severe consequences when acting on such impulses and realizing that I truly care for the one I am with. I also think of the person I'm with being with that same person and wonder how I'd feel... which isn't very good."

"We get the same urges as straight men. Just pray and jack off."

"I occasionally get propositioned, hit on or cruised by guys that I am attracted to. It is not a strong temptation, but it is a temptation. My love for my partner and my respect for our relationship always keeps me grounded. To handle temptation, I take the compliment of someone's interest, and sometimes I fantasize about that person when I am with my partner or when I am alone masturbating."

"As of right now, he wants me and only me. We have discussed opening our relationship, but he feels opening the relationship is something we can do later when our sex gets boring. I do worry that if we open our relationship, it will be the end of it. I worry some other man may come sweep him off his feet, or me. I know right now I cannot commit 100 percent to my boyfriend so opening up our relationship could very easily be the end of it. I want it to grow to be stronger, I go onto many gay sex app sites to see what's out there and talk to older couples and see how they make it work. I do know these urges to cheat are selfish and not worth what I am being offered."

"Sure there are other attractive men out there and yes you might notice them ... ignore them! You just have to think to yourself... will giving attention to another man be worth losing the love of the one person who you want to grow closer to and potentially be with forever... Something that seems to help with this is our openness about our taste in men. We can talk about who we find attractive openly and many times jokingly. As long as we are not excessive with these comments it doesn't damage our egos. I can point out guys who are clearly my partner's type... The features and characteristics that he admires and finds attractive are typically ones that I possess, which reassures me he is still in to me."

PERSONAL PROFILE #4
James and Stockton

James, 32, and Stockton, 26, have been together 1 ½ years.

"My parents divorced when I was in 2nd grade, because they both cheated on each other. I've always been determined not to do that. I look at my grandparents as role models. They've been together for 70 years and are as happy as possible. They are each other's 'everything' and that's what I've always wanted for myself."

"To me, monogamy feels like security – emotional, mental, and physical. At least it did up until this year's Pride Celebration. That's when I found out that my partner let someone suck him off at a Pride party. It just happened and we're still in the stage of talking about it. My partner feels terrible about it and wished he could take it back. I'm trying to be forgiving and I'm cautiously optimistic about returning to monogamy. However, I'm concerned. It's still a sore spot with me – we have to figure out how to regain the trust."

"I want to be monogamous, but I'm petrified that these situations will continue to happen. Stockton is younger than me and he didn't get a chance to have flings – I'm worried I'm holding him back."

"My advice to couples considering monogamy is know each other well as it's an important decision. Be honest. Communicate. Both people need to be committed to it. If one isn't committed, then the other will likely be hurt."

Given that 25% of 290 respondents acknowledged straying, these coping strategies may not work for everyone or in every situation. Although 25% of respondents acknowledged straying, none of the participants in the qualitative survey or in the interviews offered this information about themselves – (a few did complain about their partners). Perhaps it's easier to check a box than to acknowledge a 'mistake' by writing a comment. In the quantitative survey, 18% out of 290 said it was a challenge to be honest about temptations and/or 'slip-ups.'

"Although I had believed that I was in a monogamous relationship, it turns out that my boyfriend had cheated on me with several of his friends over an extended period of time. The benefits of trust and intimacy were shattered and I contracted chlamydia and gonorrhea."

Jealousy

In the quantitative survey, jealousy was mentioned as a challenge by 23%. This was a bit surprising to us since the partners were being monogamous. Perhaps related, for some, the tendency toward jealousy is part of their reasoning for choosing to be monogamous. Jealousy and the difficulty of trusting also were identified in the qualitative survey. Representative comments:

"I get jealous of my boyfriend's connections with one or two other people I fear would be more sensible boyfriends for him than me. I think being non-monogamous would make that worse."

"We both get attention from other men for different reasons. Sometimes, it can be hard to see past that. I have, however, noticed a direct correlation of increased jealousy or anxiety when I am experiencing more stress at work. I think emotions spill out in odd ways sometimes."

Our sex life is unsatisfying

Beyond finding other men attractive and wanting variety, there were a number of participants who acknowledged their sex life wasn't satisfying. For some, it was merely a matter of sex becoming too routine.

"Sometimes sex can lack after a certain period of time. We still try to be regular or semi-regular and we try to be more inventive when we do it, talking about wants, needs, turn-ons, and turn-offs."

"There's no freedom; it's the same sexual partner; we get bored with each other. We deal with this by giving freedom to one another and spicing it up in the bedroom."

"Keeping our sex life exciting has been a challenge but not a big challenge. We make sure we mix it up and try new things and surprise one another with sweet thoughtful gestures, inside and outside of the bedroom."

"Keeping sex fresh is a challenge. We have been together for nearly 14 years. I remember a time when it was harder to suggest trying something new, such as a fetish. But, as time has gone by, we both feel open enough and know most of one another's boundaries that we have no problem suggesting whatever comes to mind."

"Sex with one person is a challenge because of the way our brain operates – we respond to variety. We push ourselves to be physically fit, which keeps the excitement – but we also try many experimental things sexually together – imagination goes a long way to keep things fresh and exciting."

15 participants spoke of differences in sex drives and/or sexual interests as the reason for dissatisfaction.

"We have different sex drives. I just realize that sex isn't the most important thing in the world, and I need to slow my roll a little. When you're with somebody, when you're committed to them, you are trying to build a life together. And you just have to accept the person for who they are and compromise. That's just life."

"I'm a little younger than my partner and I want sex more than he does. However, I know it's better to be committed to the man I love and having to wait grows my desire for him."

"Also, going so long without having sex with my partner makes me think that just having the ability to be monogamish would satisfy my sexual needs."

"Having sexual desires for other men or to experiment with things that he is not comfortable with doing. I usually just discuss these things with him but then also have some alone time to masturbate about these desires."

"I was once very promiscuous, and enjoy the pleasure of having multiple partners at one time. Group sex was something I engaged in consistently. I am happy to leave that sexual fantasy behind. When it becomes a real desire, we use dildos and other sex toys to simulate group sex."

"Sometimes I get very curious about being with other people especially girls (I'm bisexual). However, I really love my boyfriend and that is enough."

And finally, age differences and limited previous sexual experience were an issue for some.

"Sometimes I wish I'd given myself more time to experiment sexually between coming out and coupling up."

"When I was his age I was wild. I don't want him to feel like he missed out."

"I'm very sexual and hadn't really experienced much before him so I'm curious and would love to try new things. He's square and not very open about sex. Plus he doesn't really want me to top him. It's still unsettled between us, although we're working on it."

"I didn't date much before this relationship so it's hard when other people flirt but I can't do anything back. I would never stray, but the temptation is strong."

Lack of Support for Monogamy

There was only one challenge not identified in the quantitative survey, that became apparent in the qualitative survey. That was the lack of support for monogamy. Although it wasn't named by many, it was held passionately and sometimes painfully by those who wrote about it or shared in the follow-up interviews. Whether it was feeling like a misunderstood minority or having to fend off unwanted sexual advances, it was often characterized as a lack of respect for monogamy.

"Perhaps the most difficult aspect of monogamy is the lack of support we have felt from other people due to the widespread practice of "opening up" relationships."

"The most challenging aspect is having values that are viewed as old fashioned and prude. It's difficult to feel a part of a community when a majority see things differently than you and don't understand."

"We have often been asked by other gay men if we would be interested in a three-way, and explaining that we are not into that can be hard for some people to believe. I think there is this general misconception that ALL gay men are in open relationships, and that's just not the case."

"Surprisingly, there's not a lot of support within the gay community for monogamous couples. We've had to distance ourselves from a few friends who don't seem to understand that there are boundaries of what is and isn't appropriate."

"When we socialize with other gay men they automatically assume we are in an open relationship. We pick our friends carefully — finding other gay friends that are monogamous isn't that easy.

"Keeping other non-monogamous guys from trying to climb in bed with us. We have to sometimes be very forward about our relationship with other people and that we are monogamous."

Advice to others who want to be monogamous

In the qualitative survey, we asked participants for their advice to others who want to be monogamous. We had 149 people respond. Some responses contained multiple ideas. We have grouped the ideas and the percentage of people who made them.

Advice to others wanting to be monogamous. (N=149)	Percent Agreeing
Communication, communication, communication	22%
Make sure you BOTH want to be monogamous	15%
Be open and honest about your feelings	13%
Stick with it; It requires patience and work	11%
Trust each other	9%
Share fantasies & sexual attractions	7%
Respect your partner	6%
Avoid the 'gay scene'	3%
Be each other's best friend	3%

Communication, communication, communication (22%)

Communication was at the core of what many had to share about what works. Whether talking about the relationship, expectations, or moment-to-moment reactions, they all focused on the importance of an ongoing dialog about the couple's desire to be monogamous and where each individual is with respect to the relationship.

"Being monogamous can be tough at times, but also very rewarding. I'd suggest talking to your partner every step of the way to be sure both are on the same page and understand one another's feelings."

"Talk about what IS and IS NOT okay for you and your partner. Discuss rules and what you're comfortable or not comfortable with. Communication is SO key."

"Do not be naive. Make sure that you have an open dialogue and explicitly state what your expectations are. Revisit these throughout your relationship."

"Find someone who wants the same thing. Talk and talk. Share goals. Share stories. Get to know the person you are going out with."

"Have a clear vision about what kind of relationship you want and need. Focus on what will make you happy in the long run, and what your long term wishes are. Check in with your partner and be open with one another about your satisfaction in the relationship."

Make sure you BOTH want to be monogamous (15%)

15% of respondents said to make sure BOTH partners want to be monogamous. They stressed the need to be on the same page – remarking that

"It definitely isn't for everybody. Make sure it's a mutual choice. If you plan to be monogamous, then stick to it! No one wants to be that person that gets cheated on. Once you have become that person that has been cheated on, there are so many other issues that get raised once you find out."

"Figure out if you really want to be monogamous first. Is this REALLY what you want? Monogamy isn't for everyone - some people are better suited to other relationships. If you are determined to try monogamy, avoid situations where you're going to do something stupid or outside the boundaries of the relationship. And if you decide later that monogamy might not work, set an option to renegotiate terms at the start of the relationship."

"It's easier to value and respect monogamy when you can learn to think about it as a tool to learn more about yourself and your partner, instead of a way of inhibiting sexual expression. If monogamy isn't for you, you shouldn't force it. Sexual expression should be fluid. It's a personal experience. Not being monogamous doesn't mean you can't be happy and in love and trust each other."

"It is important to want to do it 100%. If you have doubts, it'll be that much more difficult to withstand your desires, especially if you are naturally flirtatious."

"Make your decision together, and make sure you're not just doing what you think others want you to do."

"It's about commitment. If you can't commit to one person, you need to express that with people you might potentially date. Monogamy is not for everyone, and that's totally fine."

"If both parties aren't in agreement, it's very difficult to compromise between monogamy and nonmonogamy. You're either monogamous, or you're not."

Be open and honest about your feelings (13%)

Many participants advised couples to be very clear about their own feelings when entering and continuing in a monogamous relationship. This advice requires honesty and the willingness to communicate, but also a certain amount of self-knowledge.

> *"First of all, love yourself. If you want to be monogamous, then you have to be strong in who you are. If you are not, it will be extremely easy to project your insecurities and doubts onto your partner. This is the fastest way to end your relationship. It's all about candid communication. And you have to know and be honest with yourself before you start talking."*

> *"Focus on what will make you happy in the long run, and what your long term wishes are. Honesty in all talks you have, even if you are fighting. If you can't be truthful, you can't last."*

> *"#1. Be honest with yourself about whether or not you are truly ready to be monogamous."*

> *"Be honest about your feelings and don't try to hide anything. Make sure that you are truly in love with the person. Know yourself and what it is you really want before you do it. Speak up - don't wait for them to read your mind."*

Stick with it; monogamy requires patience and work (11%)

11% of respondents spoke of the effort and discipline monogamy requires.

> *"Be willing to fight for it. If monogamy is truly something you wish for your relationship you can have it, but it takes continuous work and commitment from both partners. It's certainly not a 'one time' decision; you may commit to the idea once, but – in practice – exclusivity is something you must choose to live every day."*

> *"Don't think it will be easy because you will be challenged and tested but it will always pay off with love and the support."*

> *"It is challenging to keep a monogamous relation BUT it is highly possible. The pride you feel about your relationship when you are in a serious and long term monogamous relationship will make you feel that love you long for from another human being. Everyone will respect your decision of a fully committed relationship."*

"It may be hard sometimes but think of the guilt that you would have afterword and having to deal with the lies. The reward is much better."

"Take the time to work on your relationship. If you really want it, you'll do whatever you need to keep it. Always try and motivate each other, don't just give up right away. Forever is a long time and between now and then lots can happen, so don't waste your boyfriend's time or your own by giving up so easily. Patience is a virtue and love is a journey."

Trust each other (9%)

9% of respondents commented on the need to actively trust your partner.

"Trust is always key. If there is ever a moment where trust falters in a relationship you have to work to rebuild or maintain that trust. Adding another man into the mix will only begin to tear away at the solid foundation that has been built. If there is no solid foundation to begin with the cracks will destroy the relationship."

"Trust and communication are really the key. I struggle with them sometimes and I can tell that it affects my relationship as well as my own mental state."

"Trust each other. Love each other. Be there for each other."

Share fantasies and sexual attractions (7%)

We heard this repeatedly in various parts of the survey. Talk openly about attractions and share fantasies – intimacy requires authenticity and is fueled by creativity.

"Talk. Be honest about where you are comfortable and what situations make you uncomfortable. Allow yourself to experience new things and allow yourself and your partner to talk about fantasies and the boundaries associated with such fantasies."

"Communicate. We have no problems discussing other people, even going so far as to speculate about someone and how they are in bed. It can be a form of foreplay."

"Instead of trying to be in an open relationship or cheating, one great way to avoid the need for other lovers is to spice it up in bed. Know their wants, needs, fantasies, and desires like your own; make their pleasure your pleasure."

"Explore your sexualities together. Be open to trying new things. If you want to try something, don't assume your partner wouldn't be interested, even if they said something before. My boyfriend said at some point he would never want to use a dildo, but right now I am working on the other side of the country, and he's using a dildo on Facetime."

"Keep a little bit of mystery, dress up for your partner like you would when you first started dating. Once you let it fizzle, it's hard to get that spark back."

Respect your partner (6%)

6% of respondents spoke of respect and consideration as being critical.

"Never take your partner for granted, small gestures of appreciation and affection go a long way."

"Respect each other and learn to love all the imperfections, as well as everything that is perfect about your lover."

"Be willing to see and try things from your partner's perspective. Expand your mind and open your heart to this one person. The ultimate goal is to spend the rest of your life with him, so be honest, be kind, be patient, be respectful."

"Take into consideration your partner's feelings. You have to be true to yourself, but if you have feelings for your partner, then do everything in your power to keep him happy and do nothing that would bring him suffering. Relationships are a 50-50 deal. So, my advice is two-fold: CONSIDERATION and COMPROMISE. Do not let yourself get walked on, but compromise none-the-less."

Avoid the 'gay scene' (3%)

A few recommended avoiding the 'gay scene' as a way of avoiding temptation, as well as common values that may not support staying faithful.

Stop trying to fit into 'gay culture' and be your true selves. So many give up on monogamy because it is hard to find in the gay scene, and isn't well accepted. There are other places to find friends, and not all of them have to be gay. Be human, not a stereotype or a member of a clique."

"Take yourself away from the gay scene with all its drama and pretense. Put your time into work and your relationship."

""Don't download Grindr. Why tempt yourself?"

Be each other's best friend (3%)

3% of respondents reminded couples that being best friends is part of the foundation.

"Don't get caught up in being their significant other, be their best friend too!"

"Above all else, make sure that you are dating someone that you would be willing to consider one of your best friends."

"Be each other's best friends. Find common interests and stay active."

PERSONAL PROFILE #5
Andy and Stuart

Andy is 39 and Stuart is 50. They've been together 4 years.

"We each had a strong preference for monogamy. It wasn't explicitly discussed, but it became self-evident. We did have a discussion when he did something that made me insecure and we talked through the terms. For me, it's driven out of insecurity. My self-esteem is somewhat fragile. Non-monogamy would be extremely stressful and hard for me to deal with. If I perceived Stuart was positively reacting to a 3rd person, it would affect me and bleed over into the relationship. Stuart has his own reasons for wanting monogamy. He has a history of addiction including sex addiction. He's careful about exposing himself to situations where he would get a rush and get himself in trouble again."

"Stuart was a former model and highly promiscuous. I never did all of that. In my head, I feel like I missed out on something – adolescence with the drama and self-discovery. I wonder what it would have been like. I'm envious of him and others who had that wild adolescent experience."

"Sexually, I get better with time – I become more confident. Stuart brings his A game from the start, but then becomes more inhibited. He wants to be in control and I'm becoming more assertive because now I'm more confident. We have to figure out how I can do new things that don't make him uncomfortable as my range broadens. It's not always easy, but the challenge is interesting. For example, how can I top him, but let him be in control? I also think that communication can be helpful – give me clues. Bringing all the facets of our personalities forward without judgment allows sex, monogamy, and the relationship to flourish. We recognize that people are not static. What creeped you out at one point might excite you now."

"Religion hasn't shaped my views toward monogamy, but race may have. The Asian-American community is more socially traditional. More importantly, if I had been born beautiful, handsome, sexy, and white, instead of Asian, I would have had a different experience and I might have chosen a different path."

"When you choose to be monogamous you're choosing to orient yourself around that one person and being mindful of going deep, rather than tasting all the varieties. My advice is 'Be there in the moment and appreciate what is going on and don't become complacent.' Men aren't necessarily wired to be this way. Monogamy has to be a conscious choice."

Chapter 4
Monogamish Relationships

"The millennials are optimistic about monogamy. However, real life intervenes, and we've become monogamish."

How do you define 'monogamish'?

The term 'monogamish' was originally coined by acerbic sex columnist, Dan Savage. Dan used the term to describe couples who are perceived to be monogamous, who are mostly monogamous, but who aren't 100% monogamous. Such couples have an expressed understanding that allows for some amount of sexual contact outside the relationship. Partners give each other wiggle room when it comes to the terms of their fidelity.

Savage believes that of all the couples people think are 100% monogamous, a lot of them are more monogamish than people realize. In fact, "A lot of people out there are in a monogamish relationship and don't even realize it."

"People simply are not always wired to be monogamous creatures." The benefits of this arrangement, according to Dan, are realism, along with occasional allowance for sexual adventures alone or with another partner.

Some of the appeal of the term 'monogamish' may stem from its vagueness – people fill in their own meaning. We had respondents use 'monogamish' in many ways. For some, it was a way of creating a 'safety net', (some critical observers viewed it as a euphemism for cheating).

"We're monogamous, but understanding if one of us slips up. Sex with someone else is not grounds for us breaking up by any means, but we're also not actively seeking out other partners. An emotional affair (e.g., going on a date with someone else) would hurt much more than a one-off drunken sexual encounter."

"When my partner and I first started to be non-monogamous, we were perhaps monogamish. The way that Dan Savage presented it, I found that it gives you an escape door for couples. This is a way to describe a mistake or where forgiveness is required. However, it may be a mile marker to non-monogamy. Whether your relationship can handle non-monogamy is another question. Can you handle the stress of non-monogamy? Is it possible to deal with all of the issues that it might bring up?"

"We have friends across the spectrum. Our younger friends all want the 'white picket fence' and then they get disenchanted and sometimes bitter. We do have friends who are monogamous and legitimately so. And then we have friends that are monogamish. That means they consider themselves monogamous, but they go out sometimes but don't tell their partner."

More typical would be a self-described 'monogamish' couple allowing an occasional 'three-way.'

> *"My boyfriend and I have discussed this several times in the past, but it does not come up very often in conversation. We both feel the desire to have others involved in our sex life, but not without our significant other. We have had other men in bed with us, multiple times, but it has never been a common thing."*

The term 'monogamish' suggests a certain ambiguity, but by doing so, it seems to invite confusion.

> *"I define monogamy as being totally exclusive with each other with NO outside sex. People sometimes use the term 'monogamish' and I think they tend to have very strict rules, e.g. they only allow oral sex or they only play with outsiders as a couple."*

> *"We hear the term 'monogamish' a lot. Our friends and us think it's kind of a joke. Either you're monogamous or you aren't. I hear the term more from straight friends. I think gays are more open to expressing that they're non-monogamous."*

> *"We constantly have conversations about monogamish and the differences in sex. There's the act of fucking, which requires no attachment. And there's making love, something we restrict to our relationship only. More than semantic, it's an attempt to clarify our desires for healthy sexual expression on our own terms."*

Despite, or because of its ambiguity, 'monogamish' seems to have appeal and an energy around it that suggests it is an important, emerging trend. Whether or not one uses the term 'monogamish', what is clear is there are a significant number of couples that consider themselves monogamous, but who allow involvement with outsiders in some form.

Having become aware of this trend as a result of written comments in our quantitative survey, when we conducted our qualitative survey, we had respondents identify as:

- Monogamous,
- Non-monogamous, or
- Monogamous but held 'loosely'–'Monogamish'

Monogamish – ways you've included outside sex?

75% of our 45 'monogamish' respondents reported mostly having three-ways and always playing together as a couple. A few couples mentioned sex parties and bathhouses, but were clear they always played together.

"We occasionally engage in sexual activities with other men outside the relationship. This sometimes includes bringing other men into the bedroom to participate in voyeuristic entertainment."

"We've had our share of 3-somes and trips to the bath house but we have never played separately from each other and are always safely together."

"We have a couple of profiles Grindr that we use to bring in the occasional third/fourth person. We don't do it very often, but we have had one-time flings. We'd like to find one or two 'friends wit benefits' but haven't met anyone suitable yet."

"We have a buddy who comes and plays with us. My partner is a total top who is into sounding and I am versatile. We decided to find a versatile bottom who was into sounding so we could experience sexually what we wanted."

"We only have sex with other people… together. Basically as long as it's an activity we are both participating in, all is fair. It's something we only do together to enhance our own sexual relationship. We've talked about what we're comfortable seeing the other person doing, and those are the rules."

25% of respondents said they played together and very occasionally separately.

"Sex with other couples, and occasional 'get out of jail free' cards (one night stands and hook ups)"

"Threesomes and groups together. Occasionally, we play apart with the other person always being informed."

"Once or twice a year, we both get the option to have a little 'change' and cut out some of the monotony."

"It tends to occur sporadically particularly around the holidays and during summer after drinking. We also each take one week a year "off" from our relationship to experience being single."

PERSONAL PROFILE #6
Bob and Ron

Bob, 30, and Ron, 38, have been in a 'monogamish' relationship for 2 years.

"We only do 3-ways, and they are rare. We're only comfortable if we're both there. We look at it as a sexual adventure that we're both going on together. The end goal is to bring ourselves closer together, trust each other more and have fun!"

"We only have safe sex and my partner doesn't like to see me kiss someone really deeply. It's not a rule, but we like to cuddle with each other afterward."

Being monogamish has helped open communication between them. Bob has used it to look at his own feelings of insecurity and his fear of being abandoned. Ron is bi-sexual, and wants to explore with women. Although it would be hard for Bob, they are considering finding a bisexual couple.

"Being monogamish has also made our sex better. We have more sex with each other now and it's more exploratory. We've used toys and tried things we didn't do before."
"We're not sure how it will evolve. The most important thing is that we respect the relationship, which must remain primary."

Monogamish – What's Working? What's Not Working?

When we asked how it's working, 90% of the respondents said it was working, although about 15% of those acknowledged dealing with challenges.

"I am not a fan of traditional monogamy, so I was the one that initially brought up the idea. He was hesitant at first and it took a lot of talking to get to a place where we were both comfortable. But I think that it has made us more secure in our relationship over time - I don't really worry about jealousy because we are able to openly talk about our attractions, and it has helped us communicate and explore what we like sexually."

"Well, our relationship has gotten tons better since the boy toys and threesomes happened – It made me see how lucky I am to have my husband. We are open to sex with others as long as it's together."

"I find this works for us. However, monogamy is our basis, because that devotional base is how we show and receive love."

"Exploring together is working. It's important to keep an open mind."

"Having clearly defined boundaries really works, actually that's the only way it would work! We talk about our desires and fantasies and remember to keep them in the context of sex... which is different from love. I can watch my man having sex with another man and know that he loves me, he goes home with me, he shares his life with me... and we can share having sex with someone else... together."

"What doesn't work? When we forget to communicate, or take communication for granted. When we make assumptions. When we jump to conclusions, that's when we have to check ourselves and remember that this is something we do together because we love each other and want to please each other. Sex with other people is not a substitute for sex in our relationship, it's in addition to sex between the two of us. It's something we jointly do together to build our relationship. And that is something we try to remind each other of before, during and after!"

Over a third of respondents mentioned that communication was key to having a "monogamish" relationship work for them.

"Being open is working. Communication is key. As soon as someone starts hiding something, it all goes down the drain. Secrets come out one way or the other"

"Understanding desires and needs and communicating works for us. Openly expressing attraction for others as well as checking out guys together. Being open and honest about needs and desires."

"We have not found anything not working. We talk about it beforehand to see if we need to set any limits. During, we always do a quick "Are you good?" to make sure everyone is still comfortable with the situation."

"What works is when ground rules and expectations are laid out and fully communicated and understood. We both are completely honest and communicate everything that we engage in. Nothing negative has come of this, thus far."

"It works because we discuss what we are planning to do and with whom – If one of us doesn't feel comfortable with it, then we wouldn't do anything with that person. The satisfaction with outsiders is physically gratifying, but it's short-lived."

What couples found challenging varied. 7 out of 45 respondents mentioned jealousy, which was the most commonly named challenge.

"We tend to have jealousy issues when we play apart."

"Flirting on social media has created unnecessary jealousy on both sides."

"We tell each other if we've hooked up separately, but I've occasionally been less than forthcoming with details or downplayed what happened with another man if my boyfriend and I are experiencing issues in our relationship unrelated to sex that would make full disclosure have a greater negative impact than it normally would. It's a less than perfect system, but it also allows us breathing room to enjoy a modest amount of sexual freedom. My boyfriend is jealous by nature even though he's more likely to have sex with other guys than I am."

"We find that jealousy is actually minimized since sex with outsiders requires another form of trust between me and my partner. We can have sex with other people and be reassured that neither of us is going to leave for someone else because of it."

Other challenges mentioned by respondents:

"I haven't really had too many issues, although I've found sometimes when I just want to have 'us' time, one of us is too consumed looking for someone to have sex with on Grindr."

"I personally prefer monogamy, but my partner likes having sex with other people. We are trying to compromise on this. We still haven't found anything that I am completely comfortable with yet, but I still want to try."

"Sometimes people like one of us more than the other and some have tried breaking us up. We've gotten better at filtering. We look for the easy going guys and make them buds."

"Some of the boy toys got where they wanted to not include my husband and that's when it ends. He was here first and I'm not giving him up."

"Three-somes don't work for us."

"My biggest challenge is being honest with myself about my insecurities and communicating those feelings to my partner."

Monogamish – possible future experiments?

We asked about possible future experiments to get a sense of how 'monogamish' might evolve for couples. About 10% described a general openness, which they held cautiously:

"We are open to anything that doesn't disrespect our relationship to each other."

"Any and all avenues with other open parties as long as there is no prior affiliation with either me or my partner before-hand."

"We're open to considering any possibilities, but we would not want a triad/ permanent third in our relationship."

"I'm older and open to most of what he may want to do. I'm not against letting him be young; I know where he is going to end up at the end of the day."

"We're open to having it go to monogamy, poly or other arrangement. The most important thing is that we keep the respect for our relationship, which must remain primary."

55% mentioned things that piqued their curiosity that they conceivably might try. These included:

- "Going to a bathhouse together"
- "Hiring a prostitute"
- "SM/BD with a boy toy since my husband is into that"
- "A gang bang"
- "Group sex"
- "Nudist venues (beaches, etc)"
- "Gay cruise"
- "Couple swapping"
- "Voyeurism"
- "Have someone spend the night"

A few mentioned trying outside sex without their partner:

- "Asking to experiment on my own, but I know I would get too jealous if he did the same."
- "Maybe sex with other guys, but not as a three-way."
- "Just a friend to have sex with, but nothing more."

A few mentioned bringing someone into the relationship:

- "Possibly the idea of integrating someone into the relationship"
- "A third that we really like and who eventually moves in."

25% of the couples said they were content and not really looking for any more than what they were currently doing.

> "We don't want more. Within the context of our boundaries......we've done it all...together! I don't feel the need to look anywhere else for anything, because we do it all together."

> "I know I'm content with just he and I doing occasional three-ways and mainly just doing each other."

> "I don't see it evolving, but rather staying about where's it at. 10-20% of my sex is with outsiders — I don't see it changing. My partner's the one for me."

> "Maybe fooling around with someone if we go out of town? I really can't say because it's not a set goal of ours to explore out of the relationship."

> "Having a loose definition of monogamy worked for us for several years. We loved each other but were not ready to settle down. Things have changed so strict monogamy is our current, and future, focus."

Monogamish – Reasons?

We asked why couples chose to be 'monogamish.' What we heard was strikingly similar to what we heard from non-monogamous couples.

Accommodates differences

The most common reasons for being 'monogamish' were to satisfy different sexual interests, different libidos, or compensate for sexual/physical limitations.

About 10% described a general openness, which they held cautiously:

> "We've found when my sex drive is low and his is high we compromise with a 3rd — sometimes, but not often."

> "It's mostly because I have a higher sex drive than he does. However, he has to approve the boy toy or three-some and he decides when it's over or if someone steps over a line."

"I have never really been a fan of traditional monogamy. I think it puts too much pressure on a relationship to expect that one person will be able to meet your every need. My last serious relationship before this one was entirely monogamous and after that experience I realized that a traditional relationship was not really for me. Additionally, my current partner has difficulties with premature ejaculation, so we aren't able to have sessions where he tops without using toys. Sometimes I just want the real thing, or I want to tag team him, or I want to be in the middle of him and another person. These desires and communicating about them is what led us to our current practice."

"My boyfriend and I are both versatile, but my boyfriend has irritable bowel syndrome and cannot bottom often. So we opened up our relationship so that I could top as much as I needed to and he doesn't feel pressure to satisfy me in that way when he is physically incapable to do so."

"We're both very sexual people and don't get too caught up on 'possessing' each other. We both acknowledge when we see a hot guy and discuss all the dirty things we'd love to do to him. Our sex is still great and often times he's the only one who knows exactly what I like and need, but we both have our own separate desires – for example, he's into military guys and I'm into older 'daddy' types."

Provides Variety and Adventure

Not surprisingly, many opened the relationship because it added fun and excitement to their sex lives and met desires for sexual variety.

"Mainly lust. We are sexual beings who are attracted to a lot of different people."

"It really was about being partners in fulfilling each other's sexual desires. It took a lot of faith and trust to even bring it up and have the conversation about trying it. And it took a few tries to set up the boundaries, with some adjustments along the way. Being able to say, 'Nope, didn't like it when you did that', or 'Yep...that was awesome.' But we found where we were both comfortable and now it's something fun and exciting for both of us."

"Guys are hot and sex is fun and we don't want to feel like our relationship is causing us to completely miss a good time."

"We are all men and still find others attractive. It is our nature. Speaking about it and openly pursuing it is being responsible."

"Billions of years of evolution have programmed humans to go out and have sex. We are not programmed for strict monogamy. If you're open about it, and talk up front it can be fun and exciting, just play safe."

"Before we were both young, both curious and very much in love with each other. Just not ready to settle down. Within the last year, of our 7 years, we have decided to become strictly monogamous and are planning for marriage."

Keeps it fresh

Somewhat similar were comments about keeping the relationship fresh and interesting.

"We plan on being together forever and it keeps our relationship fresh."

"It allows a little freedom and breaks monotony in a relationship. As long as everything is fully communicated and understood, it's okay."

"Sexual curiosity and to form a stronger bond through this joint adventure."

"We have a complete understanding of how much we love each other. We just feel that we have enough love to share with each other and possibly one or two other people."

"We both realize and agree that as humans we are sexually interested in many experiences, and we accept this and embrace our inherent sexuality."

"Keeps life interesting. Fulfilling the desire to see my man take it and lay it on someone right. Very hot to watch. It's a shared experience."

Chapter 5
Non-Monogamous Relationships

We had 48 respondents in our quantitative survey that identified themselves as part of a non-monogamous couple. Because this number was small, we ran an advertisement with the same survey invitation in Grindr, a gay sex hook-up application. From Grindr, we received 79 responses from individuals currently in non-monogamous relationships. For this analysis of non-monogamous couples we have combined the two populations (127 respondents).

The Grindr data may skew the results slightly in that the respondents are from San Francisco, Seattle and Portland. Given the perspectives in urban West Coast cities and the fact that the respondents were utilizing a sex hook-up app, we also expect their views to be somewhat more 'liberal' than our Facebook population. However, given our primary goal here is to describe how couples are handling non-monogamy, we felt increasing the size of the population was worth any increase in 'liberal perspectives.'

Opening the Relationship

47% of non-monogamous couples were open from the beginning or within the first year. That means 53% didn't start out that way - they opened their relationships after some time of being monogamous. The timing of when couples opened their relationships varied.

- 24% opened between year 1 and year 3
- 19% opened between year 3 and year 5
- 10% opened during or after year 6

Couples describe different scenarios for how they came to the conversation and decision to open their relationship. Some understood from the beginning and some took time to consider and explore. In some cases, one partner pushed the envelope or an incident occurred that forced discussion – "I got caught and had to come clean". And some couples described it as, "it just kind of happened."

"We were more like friends with benefits, the first six months of our relationship. We both were still seeing others and things were pretty fluid. At about 6 months, we started seriously discussing becoming a couple and what we each really wanted. In my previous relationship I was monogamous and I didn't want to do that again. It didn't fit who I was – I like being flirtatious. My partner had also been in a monogamous relationship, but he had cheated on his boyfriend. For him, a perfect world would have been that I would be monogamous and he would occasionally 'slip', but not tell me. I really wanted us to be able to be honest about what we each wanted and what we each were doing. After much discussion, we agreed to be non-monogamous, but we were very cautious. Initially, he was afraid to tell me when he had gone out. He didn't want to hurt me or lose me. I was clear with him that I much preferred the truth and he's seen over time that I can handle that. It's gotten better and easier as we've gone along."

"We had been together 8 years (15 years together now) when we decided to become non-monogamous. We had never considered non-monogamy; we both come from traditional backgrounds. But we were approached by a friend we had known for five years who expressed interest in becoming a part of our relationship. We had a surprisingly positive reaction to his overture. Our relationship was good at the time, but we both liked the idea of having another sexual outlet. We knew the guy well and knew he brought different qualities or traits that we didn't necessarily both have. For example, his politics were more in line with mine and he and I did the same type of work. We saw him adding to our relationship. Although we ended up not going through with it, it got us thinking. We realized we were both polyamorous and decided that having someone else be part of our relationship was something we would explore."

"We arrived at the decision to be non-monogamous after my partner hooked up with someone when he was very drunk. I had never really had an opinion one way or another about monogamy, because I always felt that the emotional component of a relationship was more satisfying that the physical component. So when my partner told me what he had done, I didn't want to end the relationship, but instead we decided to have our encounters on the side. We have never done anything together with other people, but both of us play around with others when the other is not available or not in the mood."

"Right at the beginning, I told him I wanted non-monogamy. He was okay with that. Both of us have a history of not succeeding in monogamous relationships. We'd been in relationships that started out monogamous, but ended in fooling around and lying. We didn't want that to happen. We also enjoy the variety that comes with being allowed to have many sexual partners. We both had been around a lot already. We're just being realistic and honest. Partners-in-crime."

Are We in Agreement?

Both partners wanting to be non-monogamous is critical in being able to navigate non-monogamy.

"In my past relationships, we were 'monogamous' but I cheated and people got hurt and I felt badly. I didn't want to do that again – my desire is to be non-monogamous. But that's very threatening to many people. Fortunately, my current partner likes autonomy, so me having fuck buddies gives him some distance. He's never gotten threatened by my fuck buddies."

Of the 127 non-monogamous couples, 78% of respondents agreed that both partners preferred having a non-monogamous relationship. However, some partners have not fully come to agreement. 22% reported only one partner preferred having a non-monogamous relationship. 31% of the 128 couples acknowledged that they found their differences in wanting to be non-monogamous challenging. 16% agreed that they might possibly break up within the next 5 years due to issues related to non monogamy such as honesty, jealousy, emotional involvement or not wanting the same things.

It's clearly a discussion point in almost a third of the relationships. However, based on the comments from the qualitative survey and the interviews, the number of couples where these differences feel irreconcilable seemed small. Some difference in preference and what non-monogamy should look like comes with the territory.

There are the exceptions, where the differences are pronounced and resolving the conflict is difficult.

"I've invested in this relationship and I don't want to break up. But being in an open relationship makes me feel like I'm not desirable enough. I know I would blame him if I became HIV+. I don't want to see him with anybody because I know I will feel jealous."

"We haven't argued about monogamy, I would be willing to try a polyamorous relationship if the circumstances were right, but he would not be willing to. Therefore it's not going to happen."

The bottom line is that both partners have to find their way onto the same page. We heard this from monogamous couples about monogamy and we heard this from non-monogamous couples about non-monogamy.

What does non-monogamy look like?

One respondent commented, "There's as many ways to do non-monogamy as there are people being non-monogamous." In our first study where we interviewed 86 long-term non-monogamous couples, we were quite struck with the variety. We went into the study thinking we would find models and 'solutions' that would work for others. We quickly realized every relationship was different – with different personalities, different needs, and facing different situations. There was a fluidity to the construct. Furthermore, it often changed and evolved for couples as their comfort grew or they hit challenges that were threatening.

While acknowledging the great variety, we do think it's helpful to describe the various configurations we discovered as a way of giving readers a picture of the many choices available.

In our previous study, we found some couples only played together; some couples only played separately; and some couples did both. We placed what we were hearing on a continuum from Joint to Independent.

JOINT	← ──────────────── →		INDEPENDENT
Only play together	Primarily play together, and might play separately when they go to a sex venue together	Primarily play together and occasionally play separately	Only play independently

We heard about similar variations in the current study.

"We play more together than apart, but I have fuck buddies and my partner makes connections which sometimes turn into sex."

"Over the last 5 years we continued to be non-monogamous. It's been episodic – sometimes there's been more outside sex; sometimes less. 99% of the time it has been separate, not 3-ways. We both have had fuck buddies, although my partner is a 'once in a blue moon' guy about outside sex. When we were living apart, I had fuck buddies (friends and sex partners) I saw every couple of weeks. For the last 6 months we've been monogamous – not because we've chosen it, but we've both been very busy. My desire to seek outside partners ebbs and flows – sometimes I'm on the prowl, but lately I haven't had the inclination. We both are in agreement with this arrangement and it hasn't been a source of conflict or tension or fighting."

For some couples, a three-way may just be part of their variety of experiences. However, 28% of our non-monogamous couples limited their play with outsiders to something they only do as a couple. They maintained this as a norm and tended to see it as a firm boundary that enabled them to feel more comfortable.

"My partner and I are open to having a third, but we do not sleep with others alone."

"We only do 3-ways, although sometimes we're just plain monogamous. A lot depends on circumstances, like where we're living at the time. For several years we were in a very small town and we were essentially monogamous."

There are clear advantages to playing together, and for some couples distinct drawbacks:

Advantages to playing together include:

- We share the experience, which could be fun and enriching
- It's reassuring to be right there and know what's happening and feel like you have some influence in shaping or stopping it.
- It limits the opportunity of one person getting too involved emotionally.
- We have a say in who we do or don't do and when it happens or doesn't happen.

Drawbacks to playing together include:

- We may have trouble finding 'outsiders' we both like or who like both of us.
- We may get jealous, envious, competitive or insecure.
- We may prefer different types of sex or sexual activities.

Rules

Much like 'only playing with outsiders as a couple', there are other norms and rules that couples develop as a way of promoting some predictability and ensuring a sense of security. Often the rules evolve based on what works and as needs-desires change.

"Occasionally, we have arguments about outside sex. It usually means we need to re-visit a rule. For example, we both had sex without prior permission; so we decided we needed to update the rule."

"We had been together for 2 years, and I thought we were monogamous, but I caught an STD from my partner. I wasn't comfortable with us fooling around without being open. I brought up the possibility of us doing a 3-way on an upcoming vacation. He liked the idea and we had two successful 3-ways on vacation. When we got home, we talked and decided we would play when we went on vacations. It evolved from there. We did a three-way at home and then one time I was traveling and a situation presented. I asked my partner for permission and that turned out to be fine, so the new rule was we could play when either of us was traveling. Eventually, we shifted the rules so we could play independently even in town. It's worked well and we're good about keeping things out in the open."

Excerpt from *Beyond Monogamy* (Spears & Lowen, 2010)
"Injunctions are typically serious and impersonal but given we're gay men, negotiated agreements often had a playful edge or matter-of-fact bluntness. We'd like to share some of our favorite rules that joyfully reflect our gay sensibilities."

Ms. Manners' Top Ten List

10. You can see him as many times as you want, but you can't schedule it.
9. If they're in our bed when I get home, they're fair game.
8. If you're in love with the guy, you're not allowed to fuck with him one-on-one.
7. You can put him in the sling, but no cuddling.
6. If you bring him home and he's cute, you have to let me join.
5. You can fuck whoever you want, but you can't take him to dinner.
4. If you're in the mood to fuck someone else, but I'm horny, you have to do me first.
3. You have to spend twice as much time with me than with any of your tricks.
2. You're only allowed to date the terminally ill.
1. "The Sauna Clause": Sex at the gym doesn't count as sex.

In the qualitative study, we specifically asked the non-monogamous couples about rules. Below are the most common areas in which couples had rules:

Honesty

Honesty is foundational – a prerequisite for any rules to have meaning. Although couples have different amounts of disclosure, some basic truthful communication seems essential.

"Communication and honesty are key. No lies."

"We communicate upfront and have a conversation before we actually do anything. We like to keep in touch and want to know what will happen."

"We haven't found any need for a disclosure rule, since we generally enjoy telling and hearing about positive encounters, and not about negative ones."

"If either of us is going to start seeing someone on a regular basis, we would like to be informed."

No emotional involvement

Although it's clearly not a norm for all couples, a majority of couples have an understanding about not getting too emotionally involved. Many couples have specific rules to help prevent this.

"We avoid emotional involvement – we have rules: no dates, no dinners, no spending the night."

"We are allowed to play together or separately. The main rules concern safety and preventing inappropriate emotional attachment. 'Cuddling' with outsiders is prohibited. Since we are now in a long-distance relationship due to professional requirements, we have a no-sleepover rule as well."

"No emotional involvement allowed. The person you're playing with must understand that."

"Emotional involvement isn't ever an issue for my partner. Occasionally, I've had people that wanted to get too involved. I set the limits, and if that doesn't work, I end it."

We take priority

A number of couples described rules that emphasized their desire to put their own relationship and sex life first.

"Do it on your own time. We are not allowed to cancel on each other to be with someone else. For example my boyfriend and I usually go to a Karaoke Bar every Friday so it would not be acceptable for me to cancel that event so that I could meet one of my outside sexual partners."

"No spending time hooking up with others when time could be spent with one another."

"The rules are very simple. We don't cut into 'our-time' with outside partners. Also, our bedroom is considered "our area" so any of these encounters are not done there."

Basic courtesy

Some rules are designed to avoid hurt feelings and/or uncomfortable situations.

"No sex is allowed in the apartment when the other is home or might come home."

"Our primary rule is respect and safety for each other. He can get jealous. We just talk about it; I reassure him. I never take the lead with someone unless he's clearly sanctioned it. He's quieter than me, but doesn't want to get ignored."

"Each of us has the power to veto if we're not comfortable with someone. We've used the veto twice in 7 years."

"We have a rule that we let the other know first if we're going to be having sex with someone. For example, sending a text saying something like 'I'm over at so-and-so's house, looks like I'm going to spend the night.'"

Safe Sex

Many couples had rules about safe sex:

- "No unprotected anal sex."
- "Always play safe. Get tested regularly."

PERSONAL PROFILE #7
Randy and Jeffrey

Randy and Jeffrey are 28 and 29. They've been together 1.5 years.

"We started talking about having an open relationship at the beginning. There were lots of conversations about what we wanted and how we could do it in a way that didn't harm our relationship. We both have different tastes and we're both mostly tops. Neither of us wanted to go without or take those options away from the other."

"We mainly play together, but if one of us is traveling, either or both of us might have outside sex. If it's separate from each other, we have to talk about it and get permission. We actually use Permission Slips that we fill out and sign. It forces us to have a conversation and so we know exactly what is okay or not okay. It also limits casual or anonymous sex – it means our outside sex is important enough to us that we will explicitly get permission."

"We only allow protective sex. We're both on PREP, but we still don't allow receptive intercourse if we're not playing together. We limit any emotional involvement."

"It's important to us to separate sex from the intimacy of our relationship. We want to make sure we're not doing anything that would harm the relationship."

"Jealousy is rare because we talk about it ahead of time. Once when I had more free time, Jeffrey got upset because I was having sex while he was in a super busy work mode. We had to talk it through. It was less about jealousy and more about "You're having a good time without me. I want to be there." We don't have problems with jealousy when we do three-ways. We have different tastes but we're compatible. If he really likes someone, I will say, "Okay, it's your night" knowing I'll get a chance the next time we do a three-way. We're both adventurous in bondage and kink and it's about sex, not emotional involvement."

"Clear communication has helped avoid issues. We agree that anything outside our relationship will never get in the way of us as a couple."

Disclosure

The amount a couple discloses or wants to disclose varies. Some couples prefer sharing everything, including the details. 73% of our couples said they routinely share some information about their outside encounters. While 27% had a 'don't ask, don't tell' policy.

> "We both have fuck buddies. We give a low-down at the end of the day, so we always report what we've done. I share in general terms and he's more specific and graphic, which I like."

> "We have a rule we have to tell the other about the encounter (but not necessarily before it happens). My partner has a harder time disclosing than I do. Sometimes he doesn't reveal he's played with someone until much later. It's not like he's trying to hide it or keep it a secret – he just isn't as comfortable bringing these things up. I don't really care that much, but sometimes I remind him we have an agreement."

> "Love can be on different levels. You can love someone differently than you do your significant other. Both my husband and I constantly make sure our communication is open. We like to know what happened with each other, and we don't really "sleep around". We have a small group of friends with benefits we trust. But knowing when one of us is envious of a situation helps us understand that we need to change what we're doing or look for a way to make both parties comfortable."

> "We're polyamorous, so we're quite open and disclose everything. We use Google tools a lot. We're on each other's calendars – we know what's planned. We're on individual chats between each of us and we have a group chat for all of us. We talk a lot."

Emotional Involvement

Although some partners only have anonymous sex, 63% said that one or both of us have 'fuck-buddies', or 'tricks we get to know.' This would imply some connection, but without deep emotional involvement. 64% of respondents said they have a policy of not becoming emotionally involved with others. Having said that, 36% said one or both partners has become emotionally involved with an 'outsider.' For some couples, this is acceptable. However, 14% reported that one or both of the pair has gotten 'too involved' with someone else. In some cases this is despite clear rules. In some cases, it just happened and became a catalyst for discussion and greater discernment.

Connection Limited ⟵⟶			Emotional Involvement Permitted
Anonymous Contacts	Fuck Buddies	Friends with Benefits	Secondary Partners/ Lovers

"We haven't gotten emotionally involved. I would avoid that because it could be a problem. My partner tends to play with people that he doesn't see socially so it's not much of a possibility. Most of my sex is with friends. We have strong social ties, but they're not romantic. I was playing with a couple for quite a while. That was nice because you knew they didn't want anything more than sex."

"Awhile back, we got very involved with another couple. The four of us hit it off and we sort of paired off sexually. For a couple of months, the four of us only played together. It seemed great, but then my partner played with someone outside the 'foursome' and the other couple felt hurt. I suppose we were almost at the 'falling in love' stage, but they had gotten more emotionally attached than we had. We decided to 'take a step back.' We still see them once or twice a week, but it's rare that we're sexual. I felt it as a loss. The four of us were good friends and we got to have sex together. It was the best of both worlds. This was the first time that either of us had feelings for someone outside our own relationship. The lesson was to slow down the emotional involvement – keep it at some kind of midpoint – keep it under control."

Based on our interviews in this and the previous study, we would recommend that emotional involvement is an area worth discussing ahead of time. In our first study, we were surprised how many couples hadn't discussed this. For some couples, emotional involvement is not a concern, yet it's still worthy of a conversation so that assumptions aren't erroneously made. Monitoring 'how involved' and 'too involved' takes some conscious awareness. Some partners report being able to easily set limits around their emotional investment, while others find this difficult.

Polyamory

About 7% of our non-monogamous respondents identified themselves and their relationships as polyamorous. They saw polyamory as differing from what most couples considered non-monogamy. Philosophically and psychologically, they embraced the idea that they could fall in love with multiple partners; that this could be advantageous, and that they were open to their partnership growing into a family where there are multiple loving, sexual and romantic relationships.

One respondent saw this 'potential for deepening' as the primary distinction of polyamory. "We're only a couple currently, but we're both open to deeper connections and where that could lead. We have more of an interest in finding others that are polyamorous than finding men who are only looking for sex."

"My partner and I were involved together with a third person which lasted 2 years before he moved away for work. We're still open to bringing a 3rd partner into the relationship."

"There's two of us that are primary. We're husbands and have been together 2 years although we saw each other for 5 years before that. Together, we have a boyfriend who we've been seeing for 7 months. We weren't actively looking for a third – it just fell into our laps. Our boyfriend has a partner of 18 years. We're clear we don't want to interfere in any way with their relationship. He's slowly getting more comfortable with the situation and much closer to us."

"My partner and I are domestic partners and we live together. In addition, I also have 2 secondary boyfriends. One I've been seeing every other week for 2 years. One is in med school and I only see once a month. We all identified ourselves as poly or non-monogamous from the beginning. We divulge everything; share calendars – everything is out in the open; we're very trusting of each other. Previously, I was in a triad for 4 years. All three of us considered ourselves equals and it was a closed relationship between the three of us."

"I get something different from each person - e.g., I'm versatile while one of my boyfriends is a top and one is a bottom. My primary partner doesn't like Asian food so I have Indian, Chinese and Thai with my boyfriends."

"We are more polyamorous rather than just non-monogamous - more relationship-minded than just sexual. We've had a few types of experiences. My partner had a boyfriend for the last year. His boyfriend and I were just friends, not sexual with each other. That relationship just ended last month. Currently, my partner is dating another guy, but that's not sexual. I'm dating a guy I've known for several years and have been seeing him for 6 months."

Polyamorous respondents had much to say about their perspective on relationships and how polyamory is viewed by others.

"Polyamory isn't for everybody. It takes a lot of work. You have to be adult about your emotions and you have to be willing to talk about them. It doesn't mean you don't get jealous or envious – I think that can happen to anyone. It means being open about feeling jealous or envious – not hiding the issue. Trust is important in any relationship, but it's even more critical in a poly relationship. You have to keep it honest."

"I feel there is an important distinction between polyamory and open/swinger relationships. However, in terms of perceptions within the gay/bi male community, I think people tend to view themselves as either looking for monogamy or looking for an open relationship. There is little visibility or understanding of polyamory, the desire for emotional/relationship attachments with multiple people."

"I started a non-monogamy social support group. It's a community to talk about things – a place to come where you know you won't be judged. We're on Face-Book and we meet in person every 3 months. Sometimes we serve as a sounding board to each other; it's also a way to find friends and other like-minded people. As gay marriage becomes more prominent and there's an embracement of the hetero-normative ideal – a couple with a house in the suburbs, kids and a dog and white picket fence, it can take away our queerness. The polyamory community needs to stick together in order to feel like we're not alone. It's true of the BDSM community as well".

"What would I like people to understand about polyamory? 1) It's not all about sex. 2) It's natural to us – we have a proclivity to seek different things from different people 3) It's mutually beneficial. It's not selfish or greedy – we each want the other to be happy."

Advantages of Non-Monogamy

We asked respondents about the advantages of Non-Monogamy for them personally. Below are the results from the 127 non-monogamous couples in the quantitative survey followed by examples from the qualitative study.

Advantages of Non-Monogamy	Percent of Respondents Agreeing
Variety of Partners	66%
Opportunity for sexual acts/ types of sex that my partner doesn't enjoy	58%
Helps with differences in libido	55%
Brings new experiences, learning, friendships into our lives together	55%
Brings energy/fantasy/excitement into our own sex together	54%
It allows us to stay together even though our sex together is limited/ waning	42%

Variety

The most common response was the variety of sex partners. 66% of respondents in the quantitative study agreed with this statement and a majority of the respondents in the qualitative survey offered comments relating to variety.

> "My boyfriend and I both have a history of not succeeding in monogamous relationships. We also enjoy the variety that comes with being allowed to have many sexual partners."

> "I'm slutty."

> "It started when my boyfriend worked on a cruise ship but ultimately we realized we simply have more fun (being non-monogamous)."

> "I was fortunate enough to find two men who loved me. Instead of conforming to normal expectations and excluding one of them from my love, I've accepted both of them into my heart and have sustained a beautiful long lasting and loving relationship with the both of them."

> "Boredom."

> "I felt stressed being 'tied down' to a single person for sex, and found it completely unnecessary."

Different Needs

Respondents spoke of satisfying different sexual needs. Enabling partners to have different types of sex that they, themselves didn't enjoy was a common response (58%). 55% also said non-monogamy helps them deal with differences in libido.

> I'm a top and my boyfriend is versatile, so to satisfy each other's needs we allow outside sex."

> We both consider ourselves tops and came to the agreement that bottoming wasn't really our thing, so it was a mutual understanding to become non-monogamous. We had several conversations about it first to make sure it was truly what we both wanted. It didn't mean we loved each other any less, it just meant we wanted to have the freedom to have sex."

> "We each have certain things we like and are fine with each other experiencing this. We also separate sex and relationship."

Introduces energy, new experiences

Although 27% of respondents have a 'don't ask, don't tell' agreement, the large majority of respondents were more apt to disclose. Depending on the level of disclosure, respondents spoke of integrating their experiences into their relationship. 55% of respondents said non-monogamy brings new experiences, learning, and friendships into their lives together. For some, this was routine fuck buddies, but many couples spoke of becoming close friends with someone they had originally met sexually. Respondents also used their outside encounters to 'goose' their own personal sex lives. Some brought home new sex techniques, some used their 3-ways or stories from their partners as titillation.

PERSONAL PROFILE #8
John and Sandy

John and Sandy have been together almost 2 years in a non-monogamous relationship.

"It's easier for our relationship to exist if we can have outside sex. Sandy doesn't like to bottom much. I can go out and be a top and it takes pressure off him. It's made our sex better – less predictable. We still have the spark and it lowers stress. There' no pressure for him to bottom and no pressure to have more or less sex."

"We do have rules. No friends. Nobody super close. Don't start a second relationship – no re-occurring thing. Not more time with outsider than me. Always safe – condoms. We have to be honest and tell each other."

"Sometimes we like to know the details because it can be hot. We find that jealousy is actually minimized while maintaining an open relationship as it establishes another form of trust between me and my partner. We can have sex with other people and be reassured that neither of us is going to leave for someone else because of it. As long as we're honest and show each other behavior-wise that the other is top dog, jealousy isn't a problem. We're the main focus."

"I don't see it evolving, but rather staying about where's it at. 10-20% of my sex is with outsiders – I don't see it changing. He's the one for me."

Compensates for our limited/waning sex life together

For some couples, non-monogamy is a way to stay together despite a lack of satisfaction with their sex lives together. 42% of non-monogamous respondents agreed that "It allows us to stay together even though our sex together is limited/waning. There is a difference between limited/waning. For some, outside sex is how they are getting particular sexual proclivities met – it doesn't mean their sex life at home is waning.

71% of the non-monogamous respondents agreed they had satisfying sex with their partner. Although this is significantly lower than the monogamous couples (83%) it's still a sizable majority.

	Monogamous Couples	Non-Monogamous Couples
Our sex life with each other is satisfying	83%	71%

We also looked closely at the amount of sex, respondents were having with outside partners versus their primary partner. For some respondents, sex with their primary partner was most prominent – e.g. sex with outsiders was infrequent. 29% of respondents were having sex without their primary partner less than once a month, very rarely, or not at all.

"It hasn't had any impact on our sex life together. We both like to have sex at least once a day. We would stop going out, if we thought it was lessening our own sex life together."

For some, though, sex without their partner was much more frequent (in some cases, this is the only sex they are having). However, for the most part, respondents were having sex with their primary partner more than without their primary partner.

Frequency of Sex with my Partner	With Primary Partner	Without my Primary Partner
Once a day	9%	21%
1 - 2 times per week	42%	35%
1 - 2 times per month	23%	14%
Less than once a month	13%	12%
Never/Very rarely	13%	17%

On the other hand, 26% did say they had sex less than once a month, very rarely, or never with their partner. In this study, we didn't hear first-hand accounts in the interviews or comments from couples who no longer had sex, but we imagine some of the same type of dynamics and characteristics may be in play that we heard about in our previous study.

In our previous study of 86 long-term non-monogamous couples (Spears & Lowen, 2010), 15% of the couples no longer had sex together, but still felt very close, loving, and connected to each other. Most of these couples seemed quite comfortable with having let go of their sex lives together. They talked about not wanting to throw away the love, camaraderie, and lives they had built together because of a lack of sex. Rather than lamenting their lost sex life together, they focused on the strength and joy in their relationship and were pleased that the open relationship allowed them to carry on as sexual beings without giving up what they most valued – each other.

We Believe In It

Although we didn't ask about it in the quantitative survey, it became clear in the qualitative survey, that for some, non-monogamy just seemed to be natural – the way it should be. This is similar to how some of the monogamous couples felt about monogamy.

"I think it's monogamy that's not natural."

"Monogamy is just one version of 'commitment' and we agree we don't believe it to be necessary. We're very committed to each other, and don't see non-monogamy as something that would undermine that."

"We both believe that all people seek sex and companionship outside of their primary relationship. Many just cheat, where as we are open with our feelings and urges."

"I do not believe that how I feel about one person affects how I feel about another. When my partner finds someone else to make them happy, whether for a night or long term, I am happy that they have found something to make themselves happy."

"Non-monogamy removes the greatest 'threat' relationships face (cheating/adultery) which was problematic in my past relationships."

"I believe non-monogamy requires a greater level of respect, trust, and intimacy than monogamous relationships and the success of it within a relationship can be a barometer for many other aspects of a relationship."

Challenges of Non-Monogamy

We asked the 128 non-monogamous respondents which statements about challenges fit their experience.

Challenges of Non-Monogamy for us personally	Percent of Respondents Agreeing
Jealousy/Envy	41%
Differences in the degree to which we both want to be non-monogamous	31%
There are no real challenges	30%
Communicating honestly	26%
Communicating frequently	21%
Encourages unsafe sex	18%
Encourages too much emphasis on sex - sexual compulsivity	17%
Getting too emotionally involved with outsiders	14%

Jealousy

The top challenge was jealousy – 41% agreed it could be an issue. We asked about challenges in the qualitative study as well and jealousy was also the most common response. However, in the written comments couples spoke of it as something they learned to deal with (sometimes repeatedly). They didn't speak about it as a deal-breaker.

> "I can get jealous. I just try to breathe and remember he loves me."

> "Sometimes I have to prevent myself from getting jealous, but it's not too hard."

> "Jealousy comes up, but we try to combat that with open communication and trying to stick to the rules as best as possible."

> "My partner used to get jealous. We would talk about it. I would reassure him. And most importantly we would change any dynamic where he felt neglected. The longer we've been together, the less we worry; the relationship feels secure; he knows I'm not going to leave him."

"Early on, there was some jealousy so we created a 'veto list' – people we don't want the other one doing. We don't use it much, but we each have put a few people on the list – it gives us a sense of control."

PERSONAL PROFILE #9
Larry and Tom

Larry, 34 and Tom, 33 have been together 9 years.

"At year 5, I found out that Tom had been going out. Shortly after that I went out. After a year of back and forth, we decided to call ourselves non-monogamous."

"When we first agreed on being non-monogamous, we only did 3-ways. We weren't very successful at it – finding the right guy was hard. I'm really thin and Tom weighs 100 pounds more than me – we attract different types. We decided to try playing separately and that has worked out. We had a rule that we could only do a guy once, but we let that go. Now our rules are 1) Always play safe and 2) Don't take away any time we could be spending together."

"At first, I had trouble with jealousy. I felt insecure because of Tom's experiences with outsiders earlier in the relationship. I wasn't sure if he was as committed to the relationship as I was. Tom, on the other hand, doesn't get jealous at all. But it's different now, we're closer than ever and the jealousy has dissipated – although I can still get upset when Tom idolizes one of his tricks or insists on sharing about one of his conquests."

"Non-monogamy really hasn't had much impact on our own sex life. We still have sex 2-3 times a week and our sex is a bit more diverse now. Tom is versatile and I'm a top, so it allows Tom to top other guys."

"It's been good for us to open the relationship. It's allowed us to become more intimate emotionally – we're more honest about our desires and it's made us closer."

Do we both want it?

31% acknowledged differences in the degree to which they both wanted to be non-monogamous. (Discussed previously – *see page 61*.)

"I do not find it challenging at all."

"For the most part, it has worked great for us. The only thing we sometimes run into is guys hitting on one of us and not respecting the relationships. We're secure with who we are and what we have so we only see it as a nuisance."

"There haven't been any real difficulties aside from trying to explain to others. With the exception of this, we never hit any bumps because of our non-monogamy. The main thing that we find helpful is to be open about it. Treating it like a forbidden topic only makes it feel wrong."

No challenges

30% agreed with the statement, "There are no real challenges."

Communication

Although we heard the need for active communication espoused by nearly everyone, it still can be difficult. 26% agreed that communicating honestly was a challenge and 21% agreed they had to work at communicating frequently enough. Previous comments have emphasized the importance of communication. Honesty seems foundational for both non-monogamous and monogamous relationships. Struggling with communicating honestly runs the gamut from acknowledging who you find attractive, to admitting unsafe sex, to being forthright about the extent of sexual or romantic involvement. Interestingly, we didn't hear references in current relationships about where it was grossly lacking, but rather proselytizing about its importance and appreciation of the benefits to the relationship when it was consistently practiced.

"Opening our relationship has been a very positive experience for both of us, after a difficult initial conversation and a select few major incidents that I really don't think will be repeated. I think we both attach different meanings to our own "extracurricular" encounters, but this hasn't proven to be too big of an obstacle to understanding. I feel really lucky not only to have someone who trusts me this much, but also to have someone in my life who I can trust that much."

Staying Safe

18% of respondents listed unsafe sex as a challenge. Many couples had rules about safe sex, but this didn't ensure they always complied.

"Unsafe sex has been a point of contention. My partner isn't good at sticking to it – sometimes he doesn't use condoms. I'm better at it, but I occasionally slip. We both get tested every 2-3 months and we're both on PREP."

"I contracted syphilis once, but my partner wasn't upset. The only difficulty in this was having to explain to the doctor the details of our relationship and getting the judgmental looks from her."

"At the beginning we had the fear that one of us would play without using protection. The idea of getting HIV or infecting the other was very scary. We both wanted to have outside sex. So we decided to go on PREP. We still use condoms, but PREP allows us to be more comfortable. Being on PREP has increased our willingness to bottom in a 3 way (with protection). We know other couples who have gone on PREP and it has affected their decisions as well."

Encourages too much emphasis on sex

17% agreed with the statement that non-monogamy can encourage sexual compulsivity. Interestingly, respondents in the qualitative survey didn't identify this as a challenge. 17% agreement certainly suggests it is part of the landscape. However, it's clearly uncomfortable to talk about.

We included the statement in the survey because we observed what we thought was sexual compulsiveness in some of the 86 non-monogamous couples we interviewed in our previous study. In that study, in which partners were interviewed separately, some participants claimed it was an issue for their partner, although the partners themselves didn't surface it as such. Our hypotheses is it's a real concern for some, but it's still rather taboo to acknowledge, particularly since it is a judgment call and it can share characteristics with other addictive behaviors.

The fact that 17% acknowledged they have or have had some challenge with sex being over-emphasized or becoming compulsive is worth noting. It makes sense that continuing to seek outside sexual encounters could fuel tendencies towards sexual compulsiveness and so we see this as a serious concern to take

Emotional over-involvement

14% agreed that one or both partners had gotten too emotionally involved with an outsider. We discussed this previously (*see page 67*; also, our previous study, *Beyond Monogamy*, Spears & Lowen, 2010, has multiple examples)).

One Last Profile

We close with a profile that illustrates much of what's been said in this chapter.

PERSONAL PROFILE #10
Todd and Roger
Todd, 29 and Roger, 36 have been together for 4 years.

"My partner is 7.5 years older than I am, and we met when I was 25. I was fairly inexperienced and had been in the closet for a while. From early on, he was very concerned that I would miss out by limiting myself sexually, and he let me know that it was acceptable to him if I wanted to fool around on the side, as long as I told him. I was a little hurt by this, since I assumed it meant he didn't take the relationship seriously. He had been in a non-monogamous relationship that lasted for years previously, and I don't believe it was the cause of significant problems for him."

"Neither of us acted on this until we were on vacation and the abundance of attractive men was making me antsy. We decided to turn each other loose in the club and observe our reactions to seeing the other flirt and fool around. We quickly figured out that jealousy over casual sexual encounters was unlikely to be a big issue, and consequently, we opened the relationship."

"We play together and separately. The main rules concern safety and preventing inappropriate emotional attachment - we have a no-sleepover rule. We haven't found any need for a disclosure rule, since we generally enjoy telling and hearing about positive encounters, and not about negative ones. As I started getting a little more curious about the leather/BDSM scene, we mutually agreed to a more-or-less "vanilla only" rule with others, since this is something we want to save for a later point in our relationship. If we go out to a bar or club together, we leave together."

"Small jealousy issues do pop up from time to time, and my partner believes that because of my younger age I'm more prone to infatuation with others. One problem that is a result of my age is impulse control. I can sometimes go a bit off the deep end in "cruisy" clubs and bar environments, especially when a significant amount of alcohol or drugs is involved, whereas he prefers to remain a bit more aloof. Sexual interactions we have in these environments can sometimes lead to conflict if he feels I'm following my impulses without making enough of an attempt to include him, which I admit can happen (I'm young and not unlike a puppy chasing a squirrel into traffic sometimes). Hurt feelings can also result when he feels someone is more attracted to me than to him or on a few occasions when he felt I'd become friends with someone I had played with on my own. As for me, I struggle with a bit of envy at his level of confidence and self-control."

"Being frank about our emotions is important. I suppose I would be upset if I found out that he became emotionally involved with someone else, but I really can't imagine it happening. Likewise, I don't think I would ever forgive myself if I allowed myself to become involved with someone else."

"As for what has helped, I think it's no different from what makes a relationship strong in other respects. When problems arise, we find the ways in which we are responsible and can improve. We almost always come to a point where the "offending" party empathizes with the other, and the "offended" party usually finds that he has overreacted. I can usually tell immediately when I've hurt him and why, and I find that just showing that I'm aware of it goes a long way, and vice versa. Many of the problems have dissipated simply due to the fact that we've now seen them before and realize they are not a threat or they are imaginary products of insecurities that have nothing to do with the other person."

"Overall, our sexually open arrangement has been a positive for our relationship. It's really clarified the meaning of what we have together, and has improved our sex life with one another. We consider our ability to navigate an open relationship as a sign of its strength. We are both from somewhat repressive conservative environments, and we find that holding on to the old norm of the "San Francisco relationship" is a good antidote to what I think could be an unfortunate neutering of gay life. We both had to go through quite a bit of a struggle to be comfortable with ourselves, and we don't want to give up and conform to societal pressures that I don't believe make room for the full flourishing of gay male relationships and sexuality."

"We do believe in marriage and plan to get married next year. We expect to be together for the rest of our lives."

Chapter 6
Summary and Concluding Remarks

The most striking finding of this study is younger gay men's greater inclination toward monogamy. We see this in the overwhelming number of relationships that are monogamous (86%). In addition, 90% of the single younger gay men were seeking monogamy. This is a sea change compared to older generations of gay men (30 - 50% of relationships are monogamous)

We concur with some of the comments we heard, that as younger gay men have the option of marriage and homosexuality becomes increasingly accepted, the traditional heterosexual model of monogamy and marriage become much more viable options. Younger gay men have the option of adopting to the norms of the heterosexual majority and becoming integrated into the mainstream in ways that weren't possible before. In this study, we see them taking advantage of those options in large numbers.

We also heard a second rationale for the shift toward monogamy in younger gay men. Younger gay men are coming out much sooner and are much less likely to have the experience of 'closeted sex' or to develop the sexual patterns of previous generations where a great deal of emphasis was put on sex. One way to think about this is that younger gay men come to terms with their sexual orientation much earlier and get to experience their age appropriate adolescence as gay men. This was not the case in previous generations and it could be hypothesized that because of the furtiveness, the need for an underground sub-culture and the tremendous emphasis on sex, that previous generations of gay men tended toward prolonged periods of sexual adolescence when they finally did come out.

A second finding is the sub-set of younger gay men who consider themselves monogamous, but are holding the construct much more loosely. The notion of 'monogamish' appears to be increasing, particularly as couples are together for longer periods of time. Interestingly, there is a dis-owning of the notion of 'open relationships' which younger gay men assume are wide open, whatever goes, relationships. Open relationships are associated with previous generations of gay men and are viewed as part of the previous gay culture that is no longer necessary.

One consideration is that as younger gay men stay together for longer periods of time in their monogamous relationships, more will make a shift towards 'monogamish' or non-monogamous relationships. In our previous study of long term (8 years or more) non-monogamous relationships (Spears, Lowen, 2010), 58% of the couples didn't become non-monogamous at the outset. In this group, couples went an average of 6.6 years before opening their relationship. In the current study, only 22% of the monogamous couples had been together 6 or more years. And 49% had been together 2 years or less. So they are still early in their relationships and the likelihood of them moving towards 'monogamish' or non-mongamous relationships increases over time. This possibility doesn't minimize the strong embrace of the concept of monogamy we see in the vast majority of the couples in this current study.

Along with the shift towards monogamy is an overwhelming acceptance and adoption of marriage. 92% of single gay men expect to marry. Non-monogamous couples were as likely to marry as monogamous couples and clearly didn't equate marriage with monogamy.

A few conclusions we made as observers and authors of the study:

- Despite the myths and horror stories, both monogamous and non-monogamous couples can have enduring, healthy and happy relationships.

- Also counter to myths and assumptions, it is the norm for long-term couples (both monogamous and non-monogamous) to have enduring, satisfying sex lives within their primary relationship.

- Both monogamous and non-monogamous couples were very clear about the advantages that come with their respective choices. They also recognized that challenges were probably inevitable and looked for ways to overcome the challenges in order to make monogamy or non-monogamy work.

- We went into this study knowing that non-monogamy requires both partners to fully commit to the notion of non-monogamy. However, we were surprised to hear the exact same comments from monogamous couples. Monogamy has to be seen as a choice and both partners need to embrace the concept. Having this choice be conscious (not assumed) and discussed was recommended by numerous respondents.

- Likewise, we knew that non-monogamy requires a fair amount of work, steadfast honesty and agreement to follow the rules. We found the case to be similar for monogamous relationships. Being monogamous isn't a 'done deal', but requires on-going communication,

self-awareness, strong intention, and discipline.

- Challenges come with the territory of both monogamy and non-monogamy. It is critical that a couple sees these challenges as a given and looks for ways to persevere, mitigate problems and resolve differences. Although the circumstances and situations are very different, we found it ironic that both monogamy and non-monogamy presented somewhat similar challenges (jealousy, clarity of intention, frequency of communication, consistency of truth-telling). In both cases, the key was the willingness to accept and work on the challenges

- Honest communication was consistently the top recommendation, whether talking with monogamous or non-monogamous couples.

As study authors, we know how important communication is to non-monogamy because we had lived it ourselves. However, in this study, we heard how key communication was for monogamous couples, as well. In our previous study of non-monogamous couples, although communication was espoused by all and practiced rigorously by some, we were surprised at the number of couples who communicated poorly or infrequently. In this study, we had the opposite experience. We found the communication among monogamous couples to be quite good and on the whole, probably more consistent than what we had observed in our previous study with non-monogamous couples.

We want to close with one final conclusion. Oddly, we heard both monogamous and non-monogamous respondents complaining of the lack of support for their respective relationships. To the degree monogamy and non-monogamy can be more fully discussed in the community, the better.

Both monogamy and non-monogamy are viable. Let's provide enough information and adequate avenues for discussion, so that couples can make informed decisions. Furthermore, as a community, let's stop proselytizing our preference as 'the right way' and demonizing that which we don't embrace. We need to create norms in the community, where both monogamy and non-monogamy can be rationally discussed and considered. If we can do that, both monogamous and non-monogamous couples will feel supported by the larger community.

Choices: The Perspectives of Younger Gay Men on Monogamy, Non-Monogamy and Marriage • Blake Spears and Lanz Lowen © 2016

Chapter 7
Appendix

Quantitative Survey

Demographics - All Respondents

1. What is your current age?		
Answer Options	**Response Percent**	**Response Count**
Under 20	10.6%	61
20-25	37.0%	213
26-30	21.5%	124
31-35	19.3%	111
36-40	11.6%	67
Over 40	0.0%	0
	answered question	**576**

2. At what age did you come out?		
Answer Options	**Response Percent**	**Response Count**
During or before High School	37.7%	214
18 - 22	43.3%	246
23 - 30	16.5%	94
31 - 40	2.5%	14
	answered question	**568**

3. My partner has already completed this survey		
Answer Options	**Response Percent**	**Response Count**
Yes	0.0%	0
No	59.7%	338
I'm single.	40.3%	228
	answered question	**566**

4. Longest gay relationship I've been in:		
Answer Options	**Response Percent**	**Response Count**
3 - 6 months	20.2%	113
6 months - 1 year	13.4%	75
1 - 2 years	12.5%	70
2 - 4 years	22.3%	125
4+ years	31.6%	177
	answered question	**560**

5. Number of previous long-term gay relationships:		
Answer Options	**Response Percent**	**Response Count**
0	33.3%	187
1	33.1%	186
2	22.2%	125
3	8.4%	47
4+	3.0%	17
	answered question	**562**

6. My previous long-term relationships were:		
Answer Options	**Response Percent**	**Response Count**
Monogamous	73.1%	402
Non-monogamous	12.0%	66
Both	14.9%	82
	answered question	**550**

7. Ethnicity/Race:

Answer Options	Response Percent	Response Count
Caucasian	64.0%	365
African-American	10.4%	59
Latino	22.1%	126
Asian	2.6%	15
Other	6.1%	35
answered question		**570**

8. HIV Status:

Answer Options	Response Percent	Response Count
Negative	89.1%	509
Positive	5.6%	32
Untested/Unsure	5.3%	30
answered question		**571**

9. I currently reside in (City, State, Country if not USA):

Answer Options	Response Count
	516
answered question	**516**
skipped question	**60**

10. I am currently:

Answer Options	Response Percent	Response Count
Single	37.0%	242
In a monogamous relation-ship	44.0%	290
In non-monogamous relation-ship * includes Grindr	19.0%	127
answered question		**659**

Currently Single

1. What is your current age?		
Answer Options	**Response Per-cent**	**Response Count**
Under 20	17.8%	43
20-25	45.9%	111
26-30	18.2%	44
31-35	11.6%	28
36-40	6.6%	16
Over 40	0.0%	0

2. To what extent do you agree?		
Ratings 4= Strongly Agree; 3=Agree; 2=Disagree; 1= Strongly Disagree		
Answer Options	**Rating Average**	**N = 242**
I'm looking for a committed relationship.	3.51	
I would want any new relationship to be monogamous	3.47	
I would want any new relationship to be non-monogamous	1.59	
I can imagine agreeing to a non-monogamous relationship with the right partner.	2.07	
Depending on the length of the relationship, I might consider opening a relationship and having it become non-monogamous.	2.02	
I would be inclined to marry a long-term partner	3.66	

3. In the last 3 months:		
Answer Options	**Response Percent**	**Response Count**
I've been primarily seeing one person	10.0%	24
I've dated multiple people	8.8%	21
I've been having casual sex	23.8%	57
I've been mainly sticking to myself	45.2%	108
I split up with my boyfriend	12.1%	29

4. To what extent do you agree with the statements below:		
Answer Options	**Strongly Agree/ Agree**	**N = 242**
My generation tends to be more monogamous than preceding generations	23%	
Most couples I know consider themselves monogamous	60%	
Most of the long-term couples I know are married or likely to become married.	60%	
In my mind, gay marriage implies monogamy.	68%	
I can talk to close friends about non-monogamy	59%	
I know where to find info about non-monogamy	41%	

Currently in Committed Monogamous Relationship

1. What is your current age?		
Answer Options	Response Percent	Response Count
Under 20	5.9%	17
20-25	32.1%	93
26-30	24.1%	70
31-35	25.2%	73
36-40	12.8%	37
Over 40	0.0%	0

2. Number of years together?		
Answer Options	Response Percent	Response Count
Under 1	27.4%	79
1-2 years	21.9%	63
3-5 years	28.8%	83
6-10 years	15.6%	45
11 years or more	6.3%	18

3. Number of years our relationship has been monogamous?		
Answer Options	Response Percent	Response Count
Under 1	30.2%	87
1-2 years	21.9%	63
3-5 years	28.8%	83
6-10 years	14.2%	41
11 years or more	4.9%	14

4. My partner is:		
Answer Options	**Response Percent**	**Response Count**
Similar in age	52.6%	151
5-10 years older than me.	20.6%	59
5-10 years younger than me.	14.3%	41
More than 10 years older than me.	10.1%	29
More than 10 years younger than me.	2.4%	7

5. To what extent do you agree		
Ratings 4= Strongly Agree; 3=Agree; 2=Disagree; 1= Strongly Disagree		
Answer Options	**Rating Average**	**Strongly Agree/Agree**
We have a healthy, stable relationship	3.43	98.8%
Our relationship makes me happy/satisfied.	3.49	98.7%
Likelihood of current relationship to continue for 5 more years	3.46	98.7%
We have conflicts/arguments periodically	2.66	98.6%
We fight fairly and conflicts/arguments are satisfactorily resolved	3.08	98.7%
We have considered having an open relationship	1.60	97.1%
We BOTH prefer having a monogamous relationship	3.45	98.7%
We have had arguments about opening the relationship	1.49	96.3%
My partner and I are completely honest with each other	3.30	98.7%
My partner or I have had sexual experiences outside our relationship without prior agreement	1.72	97.7%
My partner or I have 'gotten involved' with someone else without prior agreement	1.56	97.1%
We might break up because of issues related to monogamy.	1.38	95.0%
Our sex life with each other is satisfying	3.27	98.7%

6. We usually have sex together:		
Answer Options	**Response Percent**	**Response Count**
Once a day	16.7%	48
1 - 2 times per week	55.6%	160
1 - 2 times per month	15.6%	45
Less than once a month	8.0%	23
Never/Very rarely	4.2%	12

7. For us the primary benefits of having a monogamous relationship include		
Answer Options	**Response Percent**	**Response Count**
It feels right - its the way it should be	62.2%	179
Encourages connection and closeness	63.2%	182
Encourages trust and security	68.4%	197
Minimizes conflict and hurt feelings	52.4%	151
It prevents or minimizes jealousy and envy	48.3%	139
Encourages us to attend to the sex we have together	39.9%	115
Makes us more likely to stay together	58.0%	167

8. Our biggest challenges in being monogamous include:		
Answer Options	**Response Percent**	**Response Count**
The desire for more variety in partners and types of sex	28.7%	82
Staying faithful when I'd like to stray	18.2%	52
Being honest about temptations and/or 'slip-ups'	18.2%	52
Jealousy/Envy even though outside sex is not involved	23.1%	66
Our sex life together is limited and/or un-satisfying	20.3%	58
There are no real challenges to being monogamous	43.0%	123

9. We are:		
Answer Options	**Response Percent**	**Response Count**
Domestic Partners	26.2%	75
Legally Married	14.7%	42
Intending to become Married	38.8%	111
None of the above	25.2%	72

10. To what extent do you agree with the statements below:

Ratings 4= Strongly Agree; 3=Agree; 2=Disagree; 1= Strongly Disagree

Answer Options	Rating Average	Strongly Agree/Agree
My generation tends to be more monogamous than preceding generations	2.12	96.8%
The couples I know that are near my age consider themselves monogamous.	2.79	98.2%
Most of the long-term couples I know are married or likely to become married.	2.97	98.2%
In my mind, gay marriage implies monogamy.	3.31	98.1%
If I were considering having a non-monogamous relationship, I would be comfortable talking to close friends.	2.65	97.9%
If I wanted information about non-monogamous relationships, I would know where to get it.	2.54	97.7%

Currently in Committed Non-Monogamous Relationship

1. What is your current age?		
Answer Options	Response Percent	Response Count
Under 20	0.8%	1
20-25	17.3%	22
26-30	27.6%	35
31-35	26.0%	33
36-40	28.3%	36
Over 40	0.0%	0

2. Number of years in current relationship?		
Answer Options	Response Percent	Response Count
Under 1	11.8%	15
1-2 years	15.7%	20
3-5 years	29.1%	37
6-10 years	26.0%	33
11 years or more	17.3%	22

3. Number of years our relationship has been non-monogamous?		
Answer Options	Response Percent	Response Count
Under 1	28.6%	36
1-2 years	30.2%	38
3-5 years	19.0%	24
6-10 years	16.7%	21
11 years or more	7.9%	10

4. My partner is...		
Answer Options	Response Percent	Response Count
Similar in age	47.2%	60
5-10 years older than me.	14.2%	18
5-10 years younger than me.	11.8%	15
More than 10 years older than me.	22.8%	29
More than 10 years younger than me.	3.9%	5

5. To what extent do you agree? Ratings 4= Strongly Agree; 3=Agree; 2=Disagree; 1= Strongly Disagree		
Answer Options	Agree & SA	Rating Average
We have a healthy, stable relationship	92.9%	3.42
Our relationship makes me happy/satisfied.	90.6%	3.40
Likelihood of current relationship to continue for 5 more years	85.8%	3.39
We have conflicts/arguments periodically	72.4%	2.75
We fight fairly and conflicts/arguments are satisfactorily resolved	87.3%	3.17
We have considered having a monogamous relationship	66.1%	2.69
We BOTH prefer having a non-monogamous relationship	78.0%	3.09
My partner and I are completely honest with each other	75.6%	3.13
We have a 'don't ask, don't tell' policy	27.0%	1.87
We routinely share some information about our outside encounters/relationship	71.7%	2.95
One or both of us have 'fuck-buddies or 'tricks we get to know'	62.7%	2.68
We always play together when playing with 'outsiders'	28.3%	2.12
We have a policy of not becoming emotionally involved with others	64.3%	2.84
One or both of us have become emotionally involved with an 'outsider'	36.5%	2.15
One or both of us have 'gotten too involved' with someone else	17.5%	1.69
We might break up because of issues related to non-monogamy	16.0%	1.51
Our sex life with each other is satisfying	70.9%	2.92

6. We usually have sex together (with or without outsiders):		
Answer Options	Response Percent	Response Count
Once a day	8.7%	11
1 - 2 times per week	41.7%	53
1 - 2 times per month	22.8%	29
Less than once a month	13.4%	17
Never/Very rarely	13.4%	17

7. I usually have outside sex without my partner:		
Answer Options	Response Percent	Response Count
1 or more times per week	21.3%	27
1 - 2 times per month	35.4%	45
4 - 6 times per year	14.2%	18
Less than 4 times per year	11.8%	15
Never	17.3%	22

8. For us the primary benefits of having a non-monogamous relationship include:

Answer Options	Response Percent	Response Count
Variety of partners	65.6%	82
Opportunity for sexual acts/ types of sex that my partner doesn't enjoy	58.4%	73
Helps with differences in libido	55.2%	69
Brings energy/fantasy/excitement into our own sex together	54.4%	68
Brings new experiences, learning, friendships into our lives together	55.2%	69
It encourages and reinforces honesty with each other	38.4%	48
It allows us to stay together even though our sex together is limited/waning	42.4%	53

9. Our biggest challenges in being non-monogamous include:

Answer Options	Response Percent	Response Count
Differences in the degree to which we both want to be non-monogamous	30.7%	39
Communicating honestly	26.0%	33
Communicating frequently	21.3%	27
Jealousy/Envy	40.9%	52
Differences in our desire for connection with others through outside sex	24.4%	31
Getting too emotionally involved with outsiders	14.2%	18
Encourages too much emphasis on sex - sexual compulsivity	17.3%	22
Encourages problematic drug use	2.4%	3
Encourages un-safe sex	18.1%	23
There are no real challenges	29.9%	38

10. We are:

Answer Options	Response Percent	Response Count
Domestic Partners	19.7%	25
Legally Married	24.4%	31
Intending to become Married	33.9%	43
None of the above	26.8%	34

11. To what extent do you agree? Ratings 4= Strongly Agree; 3=Agree; 2=Disagree; 1= Strongly Disagree		
Answer Options	Agree & SA	Rating Average
My generation tends to be more monogamous than preceding generations	18.8%	1.96
The couples I know that are near my age consider themselves monogamous.	42.0%	2.42
Most of the long-term couples I know are married or likely to become married.	67.6%	2.79
In my mind, gay marriage implies monogamy.	25.7%	1.96
If I were considering having a non-monogamous relationship, I would be comfortable talking to close friends.	79.4%	3.25
If I wanted information about non-monogamous relationships, I would know where to get it.	57.0%	2.66

Qualitative Survey Questions

All Participants

* 1. How long have you been in your current relationship?
  Less than 1 year
  1-2 years
  3-5 years
  6+ years
  I'm not currently in a relationship

* 2. Do you and your partner consider yourselves:
  Strictly monogamous
  Monogamous, but held 'loosely' - 'monogamish'
  Non-monogamous
  Not currently in a relationship

Strictly Monogamous

* 3. What is your primary motivation/reasons for being monogamous?
* 4. What pay-off's have you experienced as a result of being monogamous?
* 5. What do you find most challenging and how do you handle it?
* 6. What advice would you give other couples who want to be monogamous?
* 7. If you would like to share more, or, you prefer answering on the phone, please give us your email address and we will contact you to schedule a brief interview.

'Loosely Monogamous' – 'Monogamish'

* 3. In what ways have you included outside sex into your 'monogamish'' relationship?
* 4. What do you find is working and/or not working?
* 5. What other outside activity might you consider in the future?
* 6. What's your motivation/reasons for considering a 'looser' form of monogamy?
* 7. If you would like to share more, or, you prefer answering on the phone, please give us your email address and we will contact you to schedule a brief interview.

Non-monogamous

* 3. What outside sex do you 'allow' in your relationship?
* 4. What rules/understandings/agreements (if any) do you have around outside sex?
* 5. What's your primary motivation/reasons for being non-monogamous?
* 6. What do you find most challenging and how do you handle it?
* 7. If you would like to share more, or, you prefer answering on the phone, please give us your email address and we will contact you to schedule a brief interview.

Interview Questions

Interview Questions - Monogamous Respondents

- How did the two of you arrive at the decision to be monogamous? At what time period in the relationship? What were the circumstances? What was your reasoning?

- Why do the two of you choose to be monogamous? What are your reasons?

- How has monogamy shaped your relationship?   What do you experience as the advantages of being monogamous?

- What about monogamy has been most challenging for you? To what extent does it get harder or easier over time?

- To what extent has jealousy or envy been a problem? What do you find to be helpful?

- What advice would you give other couples who are wanting to be monogamous?

- What impact has being monogamous had on your sex life at home?

- The research shows a shift toward greater monogamy in younger generations. To what extent have you experienced this in talking with friends, etc.? What would you speculate is contributing to this shift?

- How do you feel about this shift?

- There is also a much smaller trend toward being 'monogamish' – being monogamous, but holding it a little more loosely? Have you heard friends talk about this? What is your perspective?

- How has race, religion, or community shaped your views on monogamy?

- What are your thoughts about gay marriage? About gay marriage and monogamy?

- Anything else?

Interview Questions: 'Monogamish' Respondents

- How did the two of you arrive at the decision to be 'monogamish'? At what time period in the relationship? What were the circumstances? What was your reasoning? Were you monogamous before that time?

- How would you define 'monogamish' or how you think about monogamy and your own relationship?

- What outside sex do you allow in your relationship?

- How do you handle this? What are the rules or agreements?

- How do you think this may evolve in the future? Are there other things you might consider down the road? What's the likelihood of you returning to monogamy?

- Why do the two of you choose to be monogamish? What do you experience as the advantages?

- To what extent has jealousy or envy been a problem? What do you find to be helpful?

- What about being 'monogamish' has been most challenging for you?

- What impact has being 'monogamish' had on your sex life at home?

- The research shows a shift toward greater monogamy in younger generations. To what extent have you experienced this? What would you speculate is contributing to this shift? How do you feel about this shift?

- How prevalent is being 'monogamish' among your friends? How is it regarded? How open are you with your friends about being 'monogamish'?
- How has race, religion, or community shaped your views on monogamy?
- What are your thoughts about gay marriage? About gay marriage and monogamy?
- Anything else?

Interview Questions: Non-Monogamous Respondents

- How did the two of you arrive at the decision to be non-monogamous? At what time period in the relationship? What were the circumstances?
- Why do the two of you choose to be non-monogamous? What do you experience as the advantages?
- How do the two of you handle outside sex? E.g. play together? Anonymous partners? Only when travel?
- What rules or norms do you have around 'outside sex' (if any)? How have they evolved over the years?
- To what extent has jealousy or envy been a problem? What do you find to be helpful?
- What about non-monogamy has been most challenging for you?
- What impact has being non-monogamous had on your sex life at home?
- The research shows a shift toward greater monogamy in younger generations. To what extent have you experienced this? What would you speculate is contributing to this shift? How do you feel about this shift?
- There is also a much smaller trend toward being 'monogamish' – being monogamous, but holding it a little more loosely? Have you heard friends talk about this? What is your perspective?
- How has race, religion, or community shaped your views on monogamy?
- What are your thoughts about gay marriage? About gay marriage and monogamy?
- Anything else?

Beyond Monogamy

Lessons from Long-Term Male Couples In Non-Monogamous Relationships

www.thecouplesstudy.com

Blake Spears & Lanz Lowen

Table of Contents

Study Overview

Although non-monogamous relationships are very common in the gay community, little research has been conducted and information about how couples navigate this terrain is surprisingly lacking. As a long-term couple (34 years), this was a journey we had taken together, without a roadmap. The lessons we learned along the way were often hard-earned and we found ourselves wondering how others dealt with this. How common or peculiar was our experience? Were there models we hadn't considered? What worked or didn't work for others?

While recognizing the uniqueness of each relationship and assuming a wide diversity in approaches, we still imagined it would be valuable to hear from couples who had 'been there'. We initiated this study to hear directly from those couples.

Study goals

The purpose of the study was to better understand the experience of non-monogamous couples and glean valuable lessons. Study goals were:

- Gather basic information about how couples handled 'outside sex'
- Identify and describe typical models and approaches (to the extent they existed)
- Identify common themes, patterns, challenges and benefits
- Record what couples had to offer in terms of 'learning'

Participant selection

We chose to focus solely on non-monogamous couples. Although the similarities and differences between monogamous and non-monogamous couples interest us, we didn't feel we had the capacity or inclination to adequately investigate both.

Participants were recruited based on two criteria. Participants needed to:

- be in a long-term committed relationship (which we arbitrarily defined as 8+ years), and
- have some type of 'outside sex' or an agreement for such.

Recruitment was haphazard. We realized we had no way of methodically putting together a random sample or even recruiting a diverse population. We found participants by word-of-mouth, canvassing gay events (Pride, Folsom Faire, etc), and 'advertising' through articles and flyers in the gay press and gay venues.

Study population

As a result of our personal recruiting, we ended up with a majority of participants that looked like us – older, white, middle-class Americans - many from the Bay Area. In 19% of study couples, one or both partners were persons of color (primarily Latino or Asian).

The Bay Area was by far the most represented geography (35 couples). An additional 13 couples were from CA (outside the Bay Area). Other American couples were from FL (6), NY (5), NV (3), WA (3), IL (2), TX (2), CO (2), PA (2) and NE, TN, LA, HI, WI, DE. Nine couples resided outside the U.S.: Australia (2), UK (2), Canada (2), Mexico, Sweden and Netherlands.

Our population was also skewed in terms of age. Our youngest participant was 33 and our oldest was 81. Average age was 51. Surprisingly, almost 25% of the couples had significant differences in age. Seven couples had age differences of 20+ years and 13 additional couples had 10+ years difference in age. The average difference in age of all 86 couples was 7 years.

Partners had been coupled from 8 years to 42 years. The average length of time together was 16.2 years.

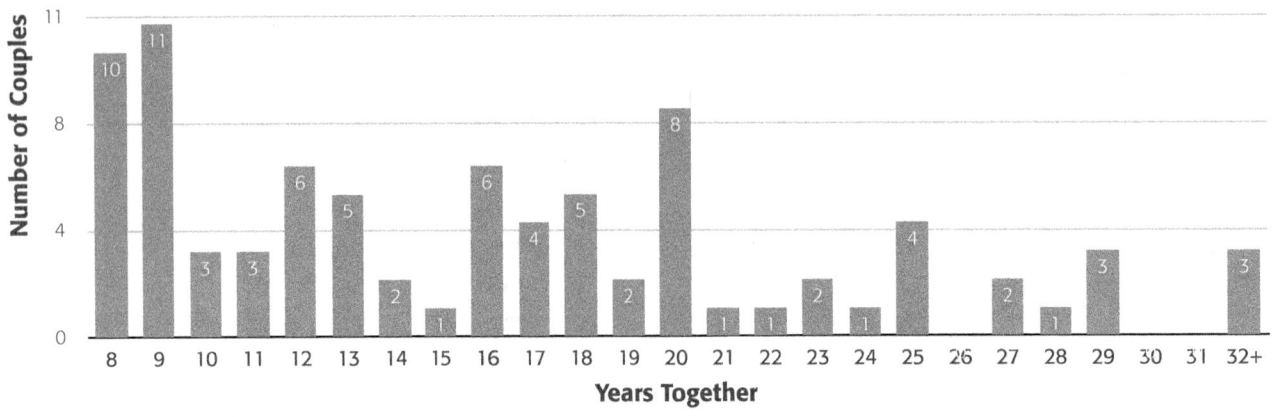

LENGTH OF TIME COUPLED

Avgerage years coupled	16.2 years
Minimum lnegth of time coupled	8 years
Maximum length of time coupled	42 years

Reluctance to participate

We found recruitment of participants difficult. We encountered a pronounced reluctance, resistance, or disinterest on the part of many 'eligible' couples for participation in such a study. We found long-term non-monogamous couples rather easily, but very few were willing to participate. Many declined immediately; some agreed, but didn't follow-through (probably typical in any study); and many reported back that their partner was unwilling. In a few instances, some couples got 'cold feet' (e.g. calling the morning of the interview to cancel; acknowledging the questions had raised unresolved issues, etc.). We can imagine all kinds of hypotheses for this reluctance, e.g. wanting to maintain privacy, lack of trust in us/the study, disinterest in the topic, as well as discomfort in talking about these issues.

Clearly our study population is not representative of all non-monogamous couples, but rather of couples secure enough to select into an interview process where they would be asked to openly focus on their relationship and the way they handle non-monogamy. Since we primarily wanted to find out what works, we figured this skewed us in the right direction – e.g. away from couples with deep unresolved conflicts, poor communication patterns, and horror stories of what doesn't work.

The interviews

86 couples participated. Each partner was interviewed separately using a consistent set of questions (see sidebar). Interviews lasted 45 – 60 minutes. 60% of the interviews were conducted in person. 40% of the interviews were conducted over the phone, (It helped that we had met 2/3 of these couples in person when recruiting). We chose not to record interviews (to protect confidentiality), but we took extensive notes and wrote a detailed summary report after each interview. Verbatim quotes were culled from the interview reports, to illustrate overall findings.

We also interviewed:
- The Center for Research on Gender and Sexuality, SFSU who have been conducting the Gay Couples Study for the last five years.
- 3 therapists who worked extensively with gay couples
- One man whose partner of 48 years was too disabled to participate
- One man whose who had lost his partner of 12 years to AIDS
- Three men whose partners ended up declining to participate

The study results, however, are based solely on the interviews conducted with the 86 couples.

Opening the Relationship

All of our couples by definition had agreement for some type of non-monogamy. Our first interview questions explored how that came about. As a starting point, we asked each partner to rate their inclination toward monogamy - when they first became a couple and currently. Results are below:

There were some obvious groupings:

- 36% were open from the beginning, with little change over time.
- 12% were slightly open and increased their openness over time
- 42% of couples were initially monogamous and opened their relationship considerably over time
- 4% were initially monogamous and opened their relationship slightly.
- 6% moved closer to monogamy and away from openness.

Surprisingly, we didn't find much difference in the 'current' rating of couples who were open from the beginning vs. couples who were monogamous at the beginning. If we only look at couples who began with an initial rating of 1 on the monogamy scale, we find their 'current' rating average at 6.2 (not much different than the 6.5

average of all couples). This would suggest that for couples who started out as open there is a fair amount of consistency over time. Their 'initial' and 'current' ratings were quite similar.

Although the couples who were initially monogamous all moved somewhat toward greater openness, five couples' who were open at the outset had moved closer toward monogamy. Explanations varied - they had consciously 'slowed things down', lost energy/interest as they aged, or felt more content with the sex they were having at home. This suggests it isn't always a one-way street. A few couples also reported that they closed their relationship from time to time.

> **Inclination Towards Non-Monogamy**
> **ON A SCALE OF 1 TO 10**
> (1=Fervent Monogamy; 10=Anything Goes)
>
> **All Study Couples**
> Initially – Average response = 3.5
> Currently – Average response = 6. 5
>
> **Couples Starting as Monogamous**
> Initially – Average response = 1
> Currently Average response = 6. 2

When relationships opened

We asked couples when they opened their relationships.

- 42% made an agreement to be open within the first 3 months, and by the end of the first year, 49% of all study couples had opened their relationship.
- The rest of the couples took from 1 year to 26 years to open their relationship – with the average being 6.6 years and the median 5 years.
- 10% of couples opened their relationship between year 1 and year 5.
- 17% of couples opened their relationship between year 5 and year 7.
- 24% of couples opened their relationship after year 7.

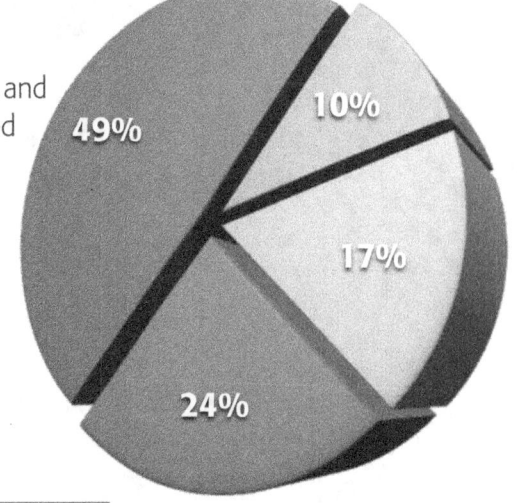

■ 49% within first year	▦ 17% between years 5 and 7
▨ 10% between years 1 and 5	▦ 24% after year 7

Opening the Relationship

Understood from the Beginning

42% made an agreement to be open within the first 3 months of their relationship. Typically, these were couples where both individuals had a strong preference for being non-monogamous based on their own personalities and desires, and/or experiences in previous relationships.

We went on our second date and Todd said 'By the way, if you're looking for monogamy, I'm not the guy.' I responded, "Oh, thank God!" Having sex outside the relationship has always been an option for us.

Jerry's former boyfriend had carried on with a boyfriend on the side, so he was very clear that he didn't want to play games. We decided right up front. "I'm gay; you're gay; You play; I'll play. Let's be realistic and open about it". We were both on the same wavelength and wanted the same thing. I had been under lock and key in a previous relationship, so I was happy to be in an open relationship.

Right after we met, I told Ted that I couldn't be monogamous even though I loved him. I just need another dick occasionally. Ted said, 'Great! I've found the man I want to be with!' We were definitely on the same page. We were open from the start, although we were mostly monogamous for the first 1 ½ years.

We knew we both enjoyed sex with more than one person. We had to decide 'How is this going to be part of our lives?' We even considered having a period of monogamy to help build the foundation, but it didn't make sense to us. We were both coming out of difficult relationships and so we started couples counseling at the outset. We wanted to understand our own motivations and hear the other's. We decided we would always play together. There was no weirdness because we both liked seeing the other enjoy himself.

Took time to consider/discover

Some couples needed a number of years together before they felt comfortable moving to non-monogamy (average of 6.6 years before opening relationship). This gave them time to develop a trusting foundation.

We were monogamous the first 5 years. For the first couple of years I don't think we ever even noticed anyone else. Then it took awhile before we got to the point of being able to acknowledge who we each found attractive. We talked about opening it up about a year before we did it. I think one of us was going on a trip alone – that became a catalyst to try it. We opened and closed the relationship a few times, depending on how we were feeling. It wasn't ever a big issue, but we've approached it cautiously and carefully.

I think that as a hypothesis I was open to it from day one but realized that it took some time to feel totally comfortable about it and not feel threatened by Ken's interest in other men, especially if I felt they were younger, fitter, or sexier than me! When I felt sure of Ken, I could be less possessive.

Eventually, there was one guy that we both liked and ended up doing a 3-way with. After that, we started talking more about opening the relationship, but I didn't know how to proceed. That was the beginning of our 'rule phase'. I was very surprised I ended up wanting an open relationship since it was different than my family's values and what I expected that I would want. It's funny – the guy we first did the 3-way with is now a good friend and we still do him occasionally

Pushing the envelope

In some cases, one partner insisted, advocated, cajoled or nudged the other in the direction of non-monogamy (14%).

When we got together, I sensed he wanted to be monogamous. He had been in other relationships and they were all monogamous. I had been in a five year relationship that was very open and that was my norm. We agreed we would be open, but he didn't really know what that meant or looked like or felt like. Two months into the relationship I happened to call him from the baths and he lost it. It was a big fight. I said if it's a deal breaker, then I'm willing to be monogamous. We decided we would be monogamous. About a year later, we were at a bar and someone hit on him and he asked me if we could take him home. We did and it was fine. For the next year, we did a lot of three-ways -- we were Dallas's premier couple looking for a third. After the first year, I introduced him to the baths. We started going pretty regularly and for the first six months we always played together. At some point I suggested we be independent at the baths. He had concerns that this would be the beginning of the end of the relationship. Since then we've gotten in the norm of going to The Club every weekend and doing people separately. That's been our MO for the last 5 years.

It took us a couple of years. Terry insisted that we be monogamous, even though I wanted to play. Terry said that if we're going to move countries and give up a career, he insisted that we be monogamous in order to make that commitment. So we were monogamous for a couple of years. In Munich, we were in a leather bar and were being cruised, and I asked Terry if we could pick up the guy. Terry gave me an 'arctic look' that said absolutely not. It took another year or two before we opened it up.

We were monogamous until 4 years ago. I could probably still be quite content being monogamous. Ted decided, rather unilaterally, that he wanted to open the relationship. I initially had feelings of inadequacy and rejection. I suppose if I had said, "This is absolutely not acceptable", he wouldn't have done anything. But, I was also curious about what he wanted and wasn't getting at home.

Rex told me in the beginning that he couldn't and wouldn't be monogamous. I had a hard time with this the first 3-4 years. I talked to a lot of friends about it, and ultimately became comfortable with the arrangement. Being open allowed us both to fully experience what we wanted to. Rex always came back to me, which reinforced my decision to allow Rex total freedom. By putting Rex's needs first and following Rex's inclinations, I experienced things that I never would have on my own, and that's allowed me to grow in ways I never expected. I'm glad about that.

Chapter 1

It just kind of happened

For some, it just seemed to show up quite organically as part of their evolution:

Albert was propositioned. We went to a movie with the guy and then we talked about it all night. We went out with the guy again and this time went home with him. He was very respectful of our relationship. We were ready to have outside sex when this guy came along. It was a watershed moment to realize that we could be attracted to each other, but also have attraction toward others. It can be hard to say what you want.

Four years into our relationship we were at the Gay Games and this guy started kissing Fred. I asked him if he wanted to invite him home. We did. Our friends were being very dishonest – saying they were monogamous, but then secretly going behind each others' backs. We wanted a relationship that was going to last. We spoke about it and decided to open it. Sex is sex; love is forever. It's an on-going discussion to some extent.

It was a gradual process and continues to be negotiated. At year 5, we had a commitment ceremony and went on a honeymoon to Cancun and started to talk about becoming non-monogamous. Soon thereafter, we started playing with others when we were on vacation -- it helped to be at ease, relaxed and far from home.

Getting caught / Coming clean

20% of study couples related periods of going out without prior agreement and having to come clean. Often the catalyst was a partner getting 'caught', followed by heated arguments and a traumatic owning up. This was not an approach any of these couples recommended.

We never talked about monogamy. The first 7 years we were both trying to be monogamous (for the sake of the other), but neither of us succeeded. Nor did we acknowledge that we weren't succeeding. At 7 years, Luke and I were having very hot foreplay - I remember it clearly. The phone rang and it was someone Luke had been tricking with saying he had been exposed to an STD. I got angry and left the house. We fought about it, but soon realized we were both 'cheating' and so it was hard to blame the other. I quickly realized, "I love you and you're the man I want to be with". We decided we could be open and moved on.

About 3-4 years ago, I walked in on Julian having sex with someone. We had a big fight and realized we both had been fooling around on the side all along. We had sex at the gym in the sauna or I occasionally met someone at the gym and would go to their house. It wasn't like either of us had affairs, it was just fooling around. Well, we decided if that's what we needed, then we should be open about it. So now we mostly do three-ways, but it's fairly open.

It was a hard decision. We only talked about it 7 or 8 years ago. We both played outside of the relationship before that, but we didn't talk about it. We each assumed the other was doing the same. The relationship began to break down (energy, time commitment to each other, feeling honest). We decided we wanted to deal with the fact the relationship was open, but do it honestly. We broke up for 11 mos. We saw a counselor the whole time. We both wanted to stay together, but we had to move the relationship to another level. The dilemma was, "How do we have an open relationship that is fair and honest and will work for both of us?" We realized that being able to go out sexually is a part of who we are and what we both want. I wouldn't be as happy without it. We needed to give each other some freedom.

We're still unresolved

In some cases (6 %), couples can't fully resolve the issue of whether or not to open the relationship. This can result in on-going conflict:

Barrett

It's always been a thorny issue for us. When we first met, I asked Ben to be monogamous, primarily because it was 1982 and HIV-awareness was rising and I was concerned about either of us seroconverting. However, Ben was very insistent that he be allowed to have outside sex and I was somewhat passive about it at first. For years 1-20, we both went out. Ben tended to have anonymous sex. I tended to get emotionally involved which caused conflicts with Ben. We still have conflict about how to handle outside sex.

Ben

I wanted it open and Barret wanted it monogamous. Even today, Barret would like it to be closed. We spoke about it repeatedly, but never came to full agreement. Over the years, Barret had a lot of outside sex, but now he's not going out. I went to sex clubs and I still have fuck buddies. There has been on-going drama because it's never really been resolved.

Leonard

We were exclusive for a few years, but then we did 3-ways. We did that for maybe five years and then it sort of stopped. We weren't traveling as much, we gained weight, AIDS became a concern, and opportunities didn't present themselves. We then had about 10 years of monogamy, although we didn't talk about being monogamous. I did phone and cyber sex, but never actually hooked up with anyone. Then once when I was traveling, I decided to go out and kept doing this when I traveled. I didn't tell Gil, but I somehow assumed he knew. This period lasted another 10 years. About two years ago, it all came out and now we occasionally have 3 ways and we have an agreement that we can go out. But it still isn't totally resolved.

Gil

Initially we travelled together and did 3-ways together when they came up. That was fine with both of us. We then went through a period of health issues. During that time our sex life diminished, but I just assumed he didn't want sex because of what he was going through. I thought we were growing as a couple, but I finally put two and two together and confronted him. He owned up to playing around on trips and that he had been for quite a while. He thought I knew. His stance was "I have to do things on my own." And he definitely wanted to keep going out. We almost broke up and we went to couples counseling. We have surfaced the issues and right now the agreement is we both can go out, but it isn't resolved. We're still in the middle of it.

What does non-monogamy look like?

When we started the study, we were hoping we might discover clearly differentiated models so that a couple might review advantages and disadvantages and rationally select a somewhat 'tested' approach. Our naiveté was short-lived. Early into the interviews we realized that relationships and approaches to outside sex were more often than not, quite different from our own, and much more varied than we imagined.

People and relationships are unique and there is no roadmap for non-monogamy. A couple has to be willing to discover their own path. Not having a model can be confusing, but also freeing. The norms aren't written in stone, so each approach to non-monogamy is organic, emergent and often iconoclastic. It has to be in order to fit the couple as they join, grow, change, mature and evolve.

While recognizing the uniqueness of each couple and their approach, we weren't satisfied with "It's a diverse panoply." We found ourselves continuing to define specific clusters in an effort to map different approaches. However, as hard as we tried, we couldn't find a way to elegantly describe the diversity. We did, however, identify what we saw as core pieces of the puzzle.

- We found three key variables that inform the 'characteristic look' of each couples' approach:
- Do they play together or independently?
- What gets shared and brought back?
- How emotionally involved do they get?

Key Variables

Joint vs. Independent
- Play separately
- Play together and play separately
- Only play together

Disclosure & Integration
- Acknowledged, but kept out of sight
- Communicated – details included
- Brought back, discussed and integrated

Connection & Involvement
- Anonymous contacts
- Fuck buddies and friends
- Deep connections
- Outside emotional commitments

What does non-monogamy look like?
Joint vs Independent

The first variable is straightforward. Couples have to consciously decide whether they will play together and/or allow each other to play independently. Each has its advantages and disadvantages.

IF WE PLAY TOGETHER

ADVANTAGES
- We share the experience together, which could be enriching (and hopefully fun).
- It's reassuring since we're definitely clued in and have influence on how it transpires
- We can limit the opportunity for emotional involvement and unsafe sex (if we want)
- We have a say in who we do or don't do, when it happens or doesn't happen, etc.

POTENTIAL DISADVANTAGES
- We may have trouble finding 'outsiders' we both like or who like both of us
- We may get jealous, envious, competitive, and/or insecure
- We may not enjoy the same type of sex as our partner
- We may not get needs for freedom, differentiation, and self-growth met

IF WE PLAY INDEPENDENTLY

ADVANTAGES
- We get to have an experience separate from our partner where we're clearly the focus
- We have much greater control over who, what, when, how
- We can experience people or pleasures that may not be of interest to our partner
- We're not dependent on our partner's health, libido, willingness, desire for connection

POTENTIAL DISADVANTAGES
- We don't get to share the experience with our partner
- The onus is on us for how & what we report back
- We may be more likely to connect or get involved emotionally
- It could be threatening to one or both of us

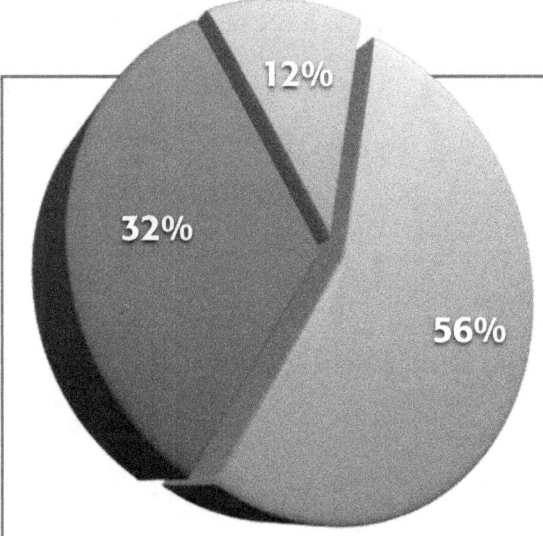

Study Couples: Joint vs. Independent

12% - of study couples chose to only play together (10 couples)

56% - of study couples chose to play together AND separately (48 couples)

32% - of study couples chose to play independently (28 couples out of 86)

31% - of the couples that did both, primarily played together and occasionally played independently

Consistency

Some couples chose an approach and consistently stuck with it for decades. This isn't surprising for couples who chose to play separately, but it also held true for some couples who decided to only play together. 50% of the study couples that only play together had been doing so since the beginning of their relationship – an average of 11 years.

Joint				Independent
Only play together	Play together unless at the same venue	Primarily play together & occasionally play separately	Play together and independently	Only play independently

Change over time

Many couples' approach evolved over time. The most typical pattern of change was couples who started by playing together and then gradually moved toward including independent play. This was often a result of the difficulty of finding appropriate 3-way partners and/or the increasing trust and comfort level that developed over time.

We didn't even acknowledge that we were attracted to other guys until 5 years into the relationship. 8 years into the relationship, we kind of impulsively decided to go into a sauna down the street. We did a 3way with someone. We decided afterward not to do it again, but several weeks later we went back. For the next 5 years, we only went to saunas together. One day, David suggested we go our separate ways in the sauna. I didn't like that, so we didn't. But we have different tastes, so it's real hard to find someone we both find attractive. Eventually we started going to saunas and doing guys separately.

The terms have changed as we've changed. We started with trying 3-ways. The first guy was a zero, but we found the experience interesting. We continued in that mode (playing together) for awhile. I stepped out once and had overwhelming guilt. I told Terry and he was marvelous about it. We re-negotiated and for awhile had a 'get out of jail free' card. If something was too nice to pass up, we would call the other and use a 'get out of jail free' card. We did that for awhile, but it didn't really make sense – if you can't reach them it's a problem and so we let that go. Now we allow each other to play independently. We both wanted our sex lives to be fulfilling.

We had argued about monogamy at the beginning. I wanted an open relationship, but he said he would be pissed off if I was unfaithful. I knew I wasn't capable of monogamy. We decided we would only play with others together. Finding people that were equally attracted to both of us was difficult. We did find one guy we both really liked and he was very respectful of our relationship. We played with him for a couple of years. At one point I was traveling and ran into one of our 'joint tricks'. I made the decision to do him alone. When I told Dwight, he wasn't upset. This was the beginning of us evolving into having outside sex separately.

We started by playing in the backrooms when we lived in Europe. Initially, we played together, but then we started taking turns going to the back room. One would tend the drinks while the other played, but we always went home together. Over the years, it became okay to go home with someone and now we sometimes will hook up online when the other is out of town.

What does non-monogamy look like?
Disclosure & Integration

The second key variable that has a big bearing on a couple's approach to non-monogamy is the degree to which information is shared and outside experiences are brought back to the relationship. If a couple only plays jointly, they share the experience as its happening. But for all other couples, choices are made on what to share and how outside experiences are brought back into the relationship. We saw a continuum between high and low disclosure and integration.

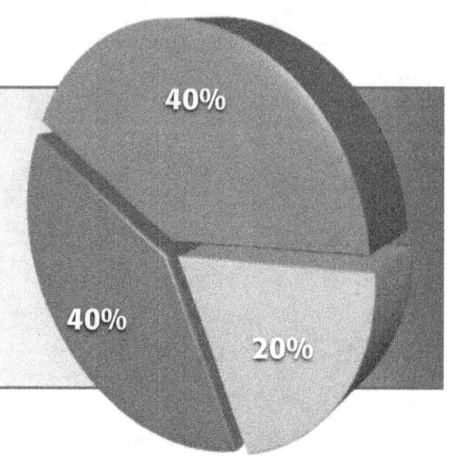

PARTICIPANTS' DEGREE OF DISCLOSURE

40% - routinely disclosed fully (including details)
40% - had varying degrees of disclosure (reported without details, offered if questioned, depended on situations)
20% - had more of a 'don't ask, don't tell' norm re: disclosure

Disclose fully

40% of study participants, who played separately, routinely report back, disclose details and share experiences. Some enjoy the process of reporting back and re-engaging. Some find knowing what happened reassuring. Some discuss the experience focusing on reactions and what it means to the couple's relationship.

I was the more insecure one and I wanted rules. I needed to know what Wayne was doing. I didn't want to find out by surprise. I wanted him to tell me. That's still an important rule.

We tell each other whatever we've done. It's not a rule. We like telling. I don't mind Pierce doing anyone, but it would hurt me if he deceived me.

Everything gets shared. It's how I can be comfortable with the situation. I'd have issues if I didn't know about it. If it wasn't discussed, it might lead to emotional disengagement. Once you start closing down sharing in one area, it may creep up in other areas. I also enjoy hearing about what Cesar has done. It fuels my fantasies.

If we split up at the baths, we share general info – Was it fun? What did he look like? Occasionally we introduce someone we've played with. We don't go into gory details or go on and on.

Our first reaction when either of us meets someone we like is, "Oh, you've got to meet my partner". We try to integrate the experiences and outside relationships, rather than compartmentalize.

There is a deeper level of honesty, trust and sharing. There aren't secrets. It's a learning experience I bring back to the relationship.

Show me what you learned

20% reported bringing back new sexual techniques and greater expertise. The experience not only gets integrated, but put to good use.

> It opens up sexual and physical ideas and options. We incorporate what we experience and learn into our own sexual repertoire.

> It's good to have sex with others. You see and experience something new and different. It gets brought back into the relationship when we talk about it. Often, when we share experiences, we say, "Mmmm, let's try that next time."

> Ted brings a lot of new ideas back. I like the variety. And it reminds us that others still find us both attractive.

> We share everything. When Jesse first started going out, he discovered that if he gave me details about what he did, then I would try those things on him. I learned a lot about what he likes and what pleases him.

> I've become a better cocksucker. Raul told me that and appreciated it.

Tell me again

The most commonly reported way of bringing back the experience was the sharing of details as a way of titillating each other. 35% of study couples described using the details to juice their own sex lives together.

> I usually want to know how big their dick was. We use it in foreplay.

> If Mac tells me and I'm titillated, then I'll ask more.

> It's fun to talk about the experience together. It's titillating. Even if we go out and don't pick up, the sex when we go home is very hot and fun. It adds an edge to the relationship. Graham's sex drive is diminishing and outside sex enhances it for us as a couple.

> I want to know. We talk about it. It helped me with my insecurity and it can enhance our own sex. I find it titillating. We also find out more about each other. "Is there anything else that he did you really liked?"

> We usually share – we find it titillating. I enjoy hearing after the fact. If I hear about it ahead of time, I get a little insecure.

Spare me the details

20% of study partners who played separately reported the encounter, but without sharing details. Another 10% said the degree to which they share depends on the situation. These couples may feel less of a need to share or may be less comfortable sharing. Some have learned how much their partner wants to hear and make choices accordingly. 10% have an agreement to only share if questioned.

We both share details at times. It's often exciting, but it can cause a little jealousy. Sometimes I filter what I share based on who the other guy is. We like to compare notes, but we definitely try to not make the other person envious.

If something funny happens, we share it, or if it's likely to be of interest to the other one. However, I like more kinky sex and Loren doesn't want to hear it, so I don't tell him that stuff. And Loren likes more 'traditional' sex, which bores me.

I don't report back what I do. Hugh shares because he wants to share. He likes to talk about what happened. I'm not a jealous type. In fact, if he tells me, I get turned on.

I share all the details although Ryan might not want to hear them. I like hearing the details from Ryan – I create fantasies based on his exploits. However, he usually just says that 'he went out' and doesn't elaborate.

When we play apart, we acknowledge that it happened, but we don't' share a lot of detail. Neither of us needs to know a lot about the other's outside activities. However, if it was a good experience for one of us, and we want to repeat, then we will discuss it and perhaps even bring the other one along.

There are some things that happen in the margins that don't get shared. There's an acceptance of unfaithfulness -that sounds harsher than I mean it - but we can read each other.

Finding the balance

A few couples talked about the difficulty they had in finding the optimum amount of information to share.

> We're still working out what we talk about. Cliff doesn't want to tell me what he does and doesn't want to hear what I did. I like sharing and the idea of not knowing what Cliff is doing is very unsettling; We've been in couples counseling the past year.

> It's been very hard for Patrick to be open about what he does sexually outside. I'm more open. Most of the change has been with Patrick becoming more open about what he shares.

> The hardest thing has been to know how much to talk about what we did outside. I tend to form relationships easier, and it can threaten George. It's harder for George to form relationships, so he sometimes sees me as being more invested in the outside relationship than I actually am. He views my relationships as more emotionally connected than I experience them.

> It's very hard for me to open up and talk about things. Talking about sex is difficult. We share most stuff – at least when it seems significant. But if he finds out later, even though I didn't think it was a big deal, then he feels like I'm not telling him everything. I doubt he tells me everything, but its okay with me.

> Tom wanting to always hear the details in order to get titillated got wearisome. I'm probably more promiscuous and I don't mind sharing some details, but it got to be too much. I had to tell him, "If you want me to be honest and tell you about what I'm doing, you can't always ask for all the little details". It begins to intrude on my own experience.

Fine distinctions

Some couples make fine distinctions about what needs to be reported:

> You have 3 days to divulge, but if it's not oral or anal it doesn't count as sex. Jacking off in the gym shower doesn't equal sex so there's no need to report.

> We do have what we call the "Sauna Clause". Basically, whatever happens at the gym, stays at the gym.

Don't ask, don't tell

At the end of the continuum are couples (20%) who agree to share very little. They have an understanding that outside sex is permitted, but generally not discussed. Some referred to this as "don't ask, don't tell".

> There are no explicit rules, but it's very limited. Any outside stuff has to happen by 6 pm because we spend all our evenings together. I guess we have the "Don't Ask; Don't Tell" policy. We don't discuss and we choose to be discreet.

> We have an agreement that it's okay to go out, but we generally don't report back. When Mack gets back in town, I don't tell him that I went out or who I played with. I suppose he could ask, but he never does.

> We still do 3 ways. We have a norm not to tell about anything else. I may see someone while he's traveling, but I don't tell him. It all feels insignificant, so it's easier not to tell him.

What does non-monogamy look like?
Connection & Involvement

The third key variable that shapes a couple's approach is the degree to which couples and partners are open to connection and emotional involvement. The continuum for this variable looks like the following:

Connection Limited			Involvement Permitted	
Anonymous contacts	Fuck buddies	Friends with benefits	Deeper connections	Emotional commitments

Avoid connections

Many couples prefer anonymous contacts. 34% of our study couples avoided both emotional involvement and on-going connections (whether out of precaution or because of their preference for anonymous sex). Many tended to see sex as 'just sex' – quite separate from love or their relationship with their partner. For others, limiting connection with outside sex partners is a way of preventing emotional involvement, something they see as potentially threatening or problematic.

We don't have an explicit restriction, but the norms we've created and the way we are each personally wired pretty much precludes emotional involvement. I can only love one man at a time and so I'm not emotionally available. I adore anonymous sex. We both have our tricks that we play with multiple times at the baths, but it's not more than that. It's, "Gee that was fun. I already have a commitment." Even when the sex is very good, I get bored after 2 or 3 times.

Nothing stated, but we both firmly believe in sex as just a release. If it were emotional, it would be much more threatening and would feel like cheating. Even now, I have some guilt that I should be home rather than out looking for sex.

We don't have any regular fuckbuddies and none of our tricks have become friends. There's a pretty strong distinction between meeting sexual needs and emotional needs. We're both men and there's that desire for variety. By being together when we play, it makes it safe/non-threatening. It's a built-in mechanism that allows us to blow off steam. We expect our emotional needs to be met with each other.

We can schedule something with someone, but not a second time. It's not a problem if you happen to run into them again, but the point is you're not planning/setting things up and seeing someone repeatedly. We're not looking for emotional attachments and we don't want them. It's a hard and fast rule that avoids complications.

It's not an issue. Sex is sex. I love Gil. Gil loves me. There is no outside emotional attachment – we're not looking, needing, or wanting.

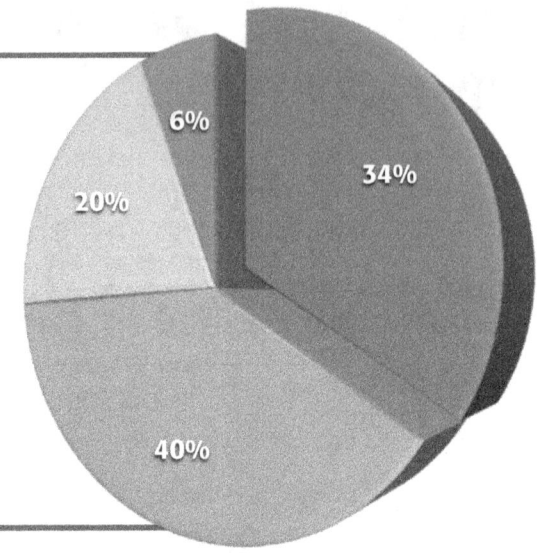

ALL STUDY PARTICPANTS:

- 34% - avoid connection - generally or exclusively have anonymous contacts

66% - prefer and/or permit some type of connection:

- 40% - typically have fuck buddies and/or friends with benefits
- 20% - have deeper connections – more than friends, but secondary to partner (includes 'above board' affairs and couples who take on temporary 'boys')
- have emotional commitments (triads, polyamorous families)

Connection allowed

A much larger group (66%) of study couples preferred or permitted some type of connection. Some couples kept the connections very limited and some couples allowed greater involvement. Connections (in order of increasing involvement) included:

- Fuckbuddies ("We only see each other for sex.")
- Friends with benefits ("We're friends, but occasionally we have sex.")
- Friends who've lost benefits ("We can continue the friendship, but not the sex")
- Friends of the couple ("We all get along and enjoy hanging out even though initially he was Tom's trick/friend.")
- Our boy ("We both love him, but not in the same way we love each other")
- Committed Third or Polyamorous Partners & Families

40% of participants typically have regular or occasional fuck buddies or friends with whom they have outside sex. 20% have deeper connections

– These include 'managed' infatuations, 'above board' emotional involvements/affairs, partners or couples who take on a 'boy' or a 'third' for a period of time, and on-going long-distance relationships that are more than friendship, but secondary to the couples' relationship.

Connection allowed, but limited

For most couples, even when connection is allowed, there is a limit. 75% of study couples had rules or norms that precluded or limited involvement. Where a couple drew the line between what's okay and what's 'too involved' varied. It depended on:

- their values
- their expectations and desires as a couple
- their level of comfort with involvement
- their level of trust in each other
- to what degree the specific 'outsider' was perceived as a threat
- the norms they had developed

Connection allowed, but limited

We're so tight and bonded that there's no room for anyone else. There's not really a chance for someone to get involved emotionally. I'm the one that is more likely to get involved emotionally since I see guys repeatedly, but they know from the beginning I'm attached. I quickly distance myself if anyone starts to get clingy or too close emotionally.

We have a clear rule that we're supposed to stop if emotions are getting involved. It's happened with me once. I had to tell the guy, "No, I'm not going to tell you I love you."

I don't think we ever had to say, "Don't fall in love with someone". Emmanuel is into anonymous sex; I'm the one that would be more inclined to form relationships. There have been a couple of people who I had sex with who became friends and became our friends (and Emmanuel had sex with as well). It wasn't a problem. I don't think I ever got too involved. Instinctually, I might pull back if I was getting infatuated. But I never felt like I was holding myself back. I think it's more that my needs are being met by Emmanuel, my family and our friends.

Neither of us wants an emotional connection. We're free to make friends and get close, but my heart is and has always been with Byron. There is a boundary between love for a friend vs. my love for Byron. I had a boy that lived in Chicago. There was some emotional attachment, but it never crossed that boundary. I was more like his father. Byron had a couple of boys too. We liked being mentors – they were a lot younger and it gave us a role and we did it together. It added to our relationship. They ran their course and moved on.

Differing preferences for connection

One of the most striking study findings was the large percentage of couples (35%) where one partner preferred anonymous sex, while the other only enjoyed sex with friends or people with whom he felt connected.

Ted doesn't like to kiss, touch, caress. He likes wham/bam, to watch, and very anonymous encounters. I like getting to know the person and touching. I want foreplay.

Brent goes after everything, but I want to know someone before I would ever want to have sex with them. Yeah, once I guess I had a bit of crush. He was really cute and really nice. I stayed in touch, but was very careful in my correspondence so that I didn't encourage anything. It passed. I don't worry about intimacy with others. I would stop myself from it. Brent? Oh he's incapable of it (laughs).

I prefer having anonymous sex. If I know their name it can ruin the experience. I've seen a few guys several times, but I don't want to become attached or emotional. I have what's called "New England emotional shutdown" – if someone is feeling an emotion, we can have a piece of cake. Tim is wired differently. He falls in love and processes like a lesbian.

We're very different people. Anyone can suck my dick, but I only kiss someone I love. I would feel embarrassed kissing someone I didn't love. Dale is opposite. Dale wants to get to know them. I just want a blowjob on the way home from work.

I lead with my emotions. We used to say that I could have a close friendship that would be as threatening as Mel having sex. But Mel's not at all jealous. I feel no restraint from Mel to rein in my emotions. There's no leash, but I stay pretty close. I feel trusted and that makes me more secure of myself.

For Ted, "It's just sex." I'm much more of a romantic – I see sex as linked to romance. The bathhouses and sex clubs never worked for me. I'd rather know something about the person – then I'm more comfortable.

Chip

Barry is more emotionally focused than me. He gravitates toward regulars. It may be a transient relationship, but for that period they're very connected. I had a couple of guys who liked me, but when that happens I get very uncomfortable. Barry would love for me to be more connected to his 'regulars'.

Barry

For me sex is love. I like guys who are emotionally available, but only to a point that doesn't require I get involved in a way that would affect my relationship with Chip.

Where's the line? Managing involvement

Having one partner open to and preferring connection was not problematic for some couples. However, for many couples there was a learning curve for each partner. The partner who preferred anonymous sex had to grapple with: "How connected does my partner have to be and what impact will that have on me/us? Will he fall in love and leave me? Will I be okay meeting and possibly hanging out with friends with whom he's been sexual?"

The partner who preferred connection had to discern, "What is the line between connection and romantic involvement? Will I be able to stop myself at infatuation? How can I follow my heart, but not hurt my partner or jeopardize our relationship?" Many couples learned what worked for them without too much drama.

I was concerned "Is he falling in love?" He reassured me. I met the guy a few times. I thought of the whole thing as Adam going thru a phase. I considered it more an annoyance than a threat. I've learned emotional involvement isn't as binary or clear cut as I thought it was.

There are no restrictions. I'm the trouble-maker on this one. Art gives me tremendous leeway. I get close to friends and like to hang out with them, but it never makes me not want to come home to Art. And if I get close to someone, I'm always open to including Art - they're not exclusive friends.

There's always that risk. There was one guy I started getting involved with so I stopped myself. There are no rules about it, but there's an understanding that our relationship is most important. Norman definitely got emotionally involved with Sam. He would just as soon have his tricks over for breakfast, but I'm not comfortable with that.

Lewis

We're primary to each other. We can depend on each other so unquestioningly. He's had a number of serious health issues and to be able to be a support to him has been really important to me (as well as to him). Walter is emotionally involved with Gene, and even I have an emotional connection with Gene. But it's very secondary to Walter's and my relationship. Our sexual relations with outsiders just aren't that important compared to our relationship.

Walter

I only enjoy sex with people I know and like. I love my friend Gene and he sometimes spends the night at our house. But I think of my relationship with Lewis as being emotionally monogamous.

Clark

Anonymous sex does nothing for me. I only get sexually aroused by people whom I know and have some connection with. So, I do get emotionally involved. It's been a minor issue a few times. . Most of our friends are people that I got involved with. Owen feels more threatened because I need more involvement. The sex usually quickly falls away and then we're usually friends, and Owen is close to almost all of them.

Owen

I don't take names or numbers. Clark gets emotionally involved and that can feel threatening. Early on, I got very insecure, but I've learned to trust Clark and the relationship. I realize I'm not in control, but I decided I have to trust that Clark and I have the same goals.

What helped couples navigate this terrain?
- Relying on their sense of trust
- Reassuring each other
- Exercising restraint
- Setting clear boundaries
- Integrating the 'outsider' into the couple's relationship (e.g. became joint friend)
- Limiting the sex if the involvement felt too threatening
- Ending the outside relationship if that was what either partner felt was needed

Going too far

While 75% of study couples had rules or norms that precluded or limited involvement, 15% with this norm had experienced finding 'the line' by going 'too far' and realizing they needed to pull back:

I fall in love. He calls it "emotional wandering" and puts his foot down. I cut it off totally, cut out the sex, or include Cliff in the sex.

We met a 34 y/o boy, Lucas, who Warren was strongly attracted to. I was attracted to him as a friend. Lucas ended up moving in with us and Warren and he had a strong sexual relationship. There was no jealousy, no drama, everyone was open. Our friends kept warning us. "What the fuck are you doing?" Their fears bothered me, but I had encouraged the situation. I was having anonymous sex and enjoying that and they were spending a lot of time bonding. Lucas lived with us for 1 ½ years, but Warren slept with me every night. I became the "Daddy" and they were the two boys. I liked that role. I felt left out and delighted. Warren's a lot of maintenance so it was a relief. We stayed the course until it was time to shift and we all agreed that Lucas needed to move out, although he's still family. We now have a different model. Warren has a handful of fuck buddies and I tell him he can have sex with whomever he wants, but he can't have dinner with them.

At first, Miles was quite carried away by Donald. It was very de-stabilizing and I drew the line. The three of us played together a few times and then we agreed that Donald would have dinner with us four or five times a week and the three of us would play once a week. We did this for a year and a half. Fortunately, Donald had a strong sense of fairness and he and Miles became much more aware of my needs. I now see it as a youthful infatuation on Miles's part.

Dating or emotional attachment would spell trouble – so we don't do it. I had one affair. We talked about it all the way through it. Bob handled it better than I did. I'm more promiscuous, but also the one that's more likely to get jealous. The affair lasted two months – it was with a married guy. At no time did it jeopardize my feelings for Bob. The guy was all over me telling me he loved me and when I finally gave in, he was gone. Bob was very supportive around my feelings of getting dumped. In the long-run, I lost my appetite for outside sex as a result of that experience. It certainly made me appreciate Bob more.

Daryle

Early on, we didn't see a person more than once. That's not the case now. Now we say "No affairs". Affair = emotional, erotic, sexual commitment that draws energy away from Elliot. We have the rule because I did have an affair at the 7 year point and it lasted 9 months. It was painful for everyone. Now, I'm much more careful to have 'friends with benefits.' If there's no romantic affair, no one gets hurt. It has been trial and error and it's still an issue.

Elliot

Daryle got emotionally involved, but now if he did, it probably would be okay because I trust that he won't leave me.

It helps if we both prefer connection

It may be a bit easier for couples where both partners favor connecting to their respective 'fuck buddies'. There's still a learning curve, but more opportunity to empathize and to join in discerning what feels appropriate and what feels 'over-the-line'.

The feeling of connection is what makes sex hot, so there is some emotional involvement. We've become friends with playmates and friends have become playmates. We both enjoy being open-hearted.

Mitch

We realize it's just sex and we save our emotions for each other. We never tell anyone else we love them - that's just for us. We have good strong feelings for our friends and fuckbuddies, but as friends. They know it's about the sex and they're respectful of our relationship.

Steven

It's never really been a problem. There were a few times very early in the relationship where I got infatuated, but Mitch called me on it and I backed off. I always look at it from Mitch's perspective – "How would I feel if Mitch did this to me?" For the two of us, the relationship is paramount.

Logan

We're very comfortable with the strength of our relationship and we're not worried about anyone taking either of us away – so there aren't any restrictions. However, we both expect to be primary. Friends or tricks could be emotionally involved, but they're more like satellites. We have crushes, but I don't allow it to go further. We understand the importance of our relationship. It's our bed I'm going to come home to.

Dwight

For myself, I'm careful not to let anything get out of hand. I learned in a previous relationship where to draw the line. I don't want to fuck up what we have.

Zak

There are no real restrictions. I have playmates I've played with for 2-3 years. Martin has met them. It's important for them to see that I have a partner. I make it very clear that I will be going home tonight. Single guys often want a relationship. I can't provide that, although they're welcome to come back to the well repeatedly. Sometimes, I have to be very clear, "That's not going to happen." I'm always quick to introduce Martin. If they get clingy, I pull away. During year two, we did have a 3rd in our relationship for about 6 months. He didn't live with us. He wanted me and we knew that, so we watched him. Martin was more suspicious than I was, but we made it clear to him. He realized the situation and moved on, although we're still friends.

Martin

They fall for Zak. Occasionally they have fallen for me, but usually with Zak because he's a social butterfly. We then have to navigate that. I don't tell him to stop seeing the person, but we talk and do confirm that they need to be reminded its physical and a friendship – not more. We let it play out, even if they're macho and think they're going to win Zak away. It's about them, not us. We don't want to lead them on or damage their self-esteem. They either get it and deal with it or they move on.

Larry

We don't have rules. We have run into only one situation. We had a visitor from Argentina – a young kid. I felt like an affectionate big brother. The three of us played - Dennis more than me. Dennis was aware I found the kid very appealing and we both knew the kid was going back to Argentina. But it turned out that Dennis felt uncomfortable and threatened. I felt warmly toward the kid and flattered that we had some type of bond, but it wasn't at all comparable to what I feel for Dennis and certainly not a threat. However, I wasn't being aware of how it might be impacting Dennis. There is a line. We do get close to some of our friends, but my feelings for Dennis are qualitatively and quantitatively different. One of the key things we believe – a third can't break a sound couple up. As long as we love each other, nothing will pull us apart.

Dennis

We're sometimes sexual with friends and some 3-ways have become our friends. We both know we're allowing ourselves to be open to others. To some degree, that puts the relationship 'at risk' but it makes us both feel free and that we're choosing to be in the relationship. Larry had a cute guy from Argentina visit and he told me how special the guy was. I felt threatened by that and told Larry my fears. Larry felt really bad that he had caused me to feel insecure.

Or is it double the trouble?

On the other hand, for some couples where both partners favor connecting with outsiders, there may be less vigilance and a tendency to allow more. Sometimes one or both go "too far".

I was concerned "Is he falling in love?" He reassured me. I met the guy a few times. I thought of the whole thing as Adam going thru a phase. I considered it more an annoyance than a threat. I've learned emotional involvement isn't as binary or clear cut as I thought it was.

There are no restrictions. I'm the trouble-maker on this one. Art gives me tremendous leeway. I get close to friends and like to hang out with them, but it never makes me not want to come home to Art. And if I get close to someone, I'm always open to including Art - they're not exclusive friends.

There's always that risk. There was one guy I started getting involved with so I stopped myself. There are no rules about it, but there's an understanding that our relationship is most important. Norman definitely got emotionally involved with Sam. He would just as soon have his tricks over for breakfast, but I'm not comfortable with that.

Lewis

We're primary to each other. We can depend on each other so unquestioningly. He's had a number of serious health issues and to be able to be a support to him has been really important to me (as well as to him). Walter is emotionally involved with Gene, and even I have an emotional connection with Gene. But it's very secondary to Walter's and my relationship. Our sexual relations with outsiders just aren't that important compared to our relationship.

Walter

I only enjoy sex with people I know and like. I love my friend Gene and he sometimes spends the night at our house. But I think of my relationship with Lewis as being emotionally monogamous.

Involvement permitted

A few study couples described situations where partners got very involved, but they were reluctant to squelch it. Even though it created tension or was potentially threatening, the partners preferred not to put constraints on each other. In these cases, everything was very transparent, discussed frequently and ultimately treated as learning opportunities

Wayne

Jim is seeing someone who he really likes and they have gone on two weekend excursions together. If there was ever going to be a threat, it's probably this guy. Jim is keeping me informed and I can tell by his demeanor that nothing between him and me has changed. He has sexual and spiritual needs I know I can't meet. He likes drugs and intense sex. I don't do either. I know my limitations and I've always been secure. It's about mutual happiness and mutual supportiveness. I'd rather us put our energy and focus on what we have and what we enjoy together. Where we don't meet our partner's needs, let them find their way and meet them. He brings his excitement back to our relationship. I never say to Jim he can't do something. I think if I denied him, it wouldn't be a good thing. I can dialogue about it, but I can't say 'No'. It may be something very important to him. I don't feel hurt by it because he's not being any different with me.

Jim

There's a guy with whom I'm getting very connected. It doesn't feel as romantic as it feels like a 'heart expansion'. We've spent two weekends together. It doesn't feel that de-stabilizing, but Wayne and I talk about it and what it means to our relationship. Wayne doesn't put constraints on me, but I put constraints on myself. Wayne is okay as long as the outside involvement doesn't threaten our relationship.

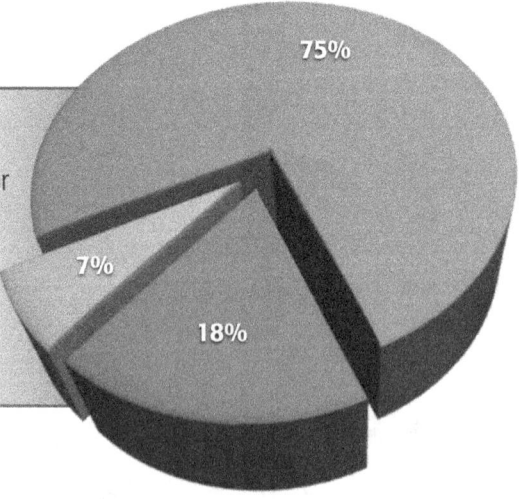

PARTICIPANTS' DEGREE OF INVOLVEMENT

75% - study couples had rules or norms that precluded or limited involvement

18% - study couples had no restrictions on involvement

7% - had never discussed the issue of emotional involvement

Getting involved as a couple

Some couples found themselves getting involved with a third – as a couple. When couples are getting connected to the same person at the same time, it may feel less threatening to the relationship. We were surprised at the number of couples (13%) who reported having 'a boy' or taking on a third for a period of time. Some of these couples clearly had restrictions against involvement, but their norm was over-ridden by their shared interest and enjoyment. Several couples stated this was an anomaly and didn't expect it to happen again. Some couples had a number of 'boys' over the years.

> We don't fall in love with anyone else, but we've had instances where we've become emotionally attached, but we've always done it together. For awhile we had a third living with us.

> We found a guy we care about and love. He's more than a trick. He's a dear friend. We both love him, but we're not in love with him. We certainly don't love him like we do each other; he's more like our boy – he's 32 and naïve. We watch out for him – have him over for dinner or to play. He is the only one we feel that way about. We'd love to see him find a relationship of his own.

> Emotional involvement is the last thing either of us would want. The only exception was with a neighbor we had 6 years into the relationship. We both liked him very much. We had many 3-somes together and he would spend weekends with us. We tried to keep him connected to both of us equally, but in the second year he became more emotionally involved with me. We ended the relationship at that point because it was hurtful to John. It was the best thing to do. We're still friends, but the sex stopped as soon as he developed romantic feelings toward me.

> We met a guy in '96 that we started to see a lot for 3 months. He was new to the area. He spent every weekend with us, until we felt he was starting to get emotionally involved. We weren't looking for a 3-way relationship and so we had to pull back. We didn't see him for a couple of months, but after that we all became friends again. Eventually, he met someone else and we've maintained our relationship with him. He was the best man at our wedding and our commitment ceremony.

Triads and polyamorous families

A small, but significant number of study couples had enlarged their relationship to include and embrace new members. They felt like they could love and 'be in love' with more than one person (some couples labeled this polyamorous). A third or possibly more people were incorporated into the 'family'. For some this was situational, "we both fell in love with him". For others, it was intentional.

Although one might assume these were couples where 'anything goes', in fact, these 'families' took considerable time to communicate, problem-solve, and build trust and commitment.

> We had a rule that there wouldn't be any emotional involvement. I used to worry that Dale would get attached if he had a really good outside experience. When we met Adrian, we both agreed that he was different. The three of us have been together for 4 years and I expect to be with the two of them the rest of my life. We're monogamous at this point (no longer have 'outside sex'). The three of us all go to therapy, individually and together as needed.

Although we only interviewed a small number of couples or families that fit this model, we talked with 2-3 times that many about participating. The model deserves its own study since the philosophy, dynamics, and issues are quite different from many of our study couples.

Joe

Thom and I were together for 5 years before we met Trent. Trent has been with us for the last 8 years. He's a senior exec at a Fortune 500 company and routinely takes us both to the company's retreats. He introduces us as his 'two husbands'. Sometimes we all do things together and sometimes it's just two of us (any two of us). Our families have been very supportive. They saw how loyal and caring Trent and Thom were when I had cancer.

Thom

I have two husbands. A stool with 3 legs is stronger. We all balance each other. I'm playful even though I have a backbone of steel. Joe and Trent are the adults. Trent is in Denver four days a week, but when we're together with Trent, we're really together. We still have outside sex and various connections, but the three of us are emotionally monogamous.

Trent

It's been a hard year with Joe's health problems. Thom and I alternated 12 hour shifts when Joe was in the hospital and he needed a lot of support when he came home. I don't know how we would have done it if there weren't three of us. It's definitely made us all stronger.

Carl

Walt is my husband, but I have two other major relationships – Chase is my 'boy'. I'm in love with him. Chase is in a 10-year relationship with my best friend. I'm also in love with Nelson, my other boy. We all view ourselves as family. Walt and I don't keep anything from each other. The 5 of us are very, very close. There are a variety of relationships, not all sexual, but all intimate.

Walt

When Carl tells me about someone new, I can't help thinking "Oh dear God, are you falling in love with another one?"' That's when Carl usually says, "I'm going to slap you if you roll your eyes again." No, I'm not threatened by it. Carl is incredibly loyal and I know we're in it for the long haul.

Leonard

I was with my ex-partner Taylor, when I met Phillip. I've always considered myself polyamorous and so for the first four years that Phillip and I were together, I was still with Taylor. The three of us got along well together. Our relationship is definitely wide open, but it's not anything goes as in 'whatever'. We're very responsible and committed to what we have. The norms we have:

- Honesty. A very proactive honesty that includes consistent checking in.

- Trying to integrate, rather than compartmentalize. If I have a relationship that is becoming serious, I need to introduce that person to the family and they need to welcome them in (or not). If they're not comfortable with the person than it won't work.

- Consideration and respect. Each of us is good about sharing time with the others. They have their own relationships with each other (non-sexual), and are respectful of each one's relationship with me.

Anything is fine if it adds to what we have here. If I (or someone else) was to get involved with someone in a way that jeopardized what we have, we wouldn't do it.

Phillip

We consciously defined ourselves as open from the beginning. Each of us is free to see others within the boundary of not upsetting the whole. My previous partners were into the drama of jealousy, which just doesn't work for me. Leonard was with Taylor when we met. The three of us became a triad. It worked really well and I was really sad when Taylor decided not to continue.

Approaches to Rules & Norms

Explicit rules are one way couples can manage expectations, behaviors, and fears. In what little research that has been done on non-monogamy, rules and explicit agreements have been a central focus. However, we found less reliance on explicit rules than what the research assumes.

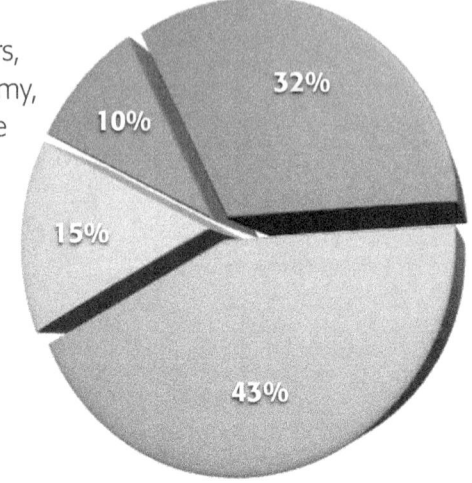

APPROACHES TO RULES AND NORMS
32% - had explicit rules
43% - had norms or understandings
15% - had very fluid, emergent rules
10% - eschewed rules

No rules

In fact, 10% of our study couples were explicitly disdainful of rules:

> I wouldn't be comfortable with a bunch of rules. You'd be constantly watching out for the rules and whose breaking them and then you would have to punish them. Who wants to focus on any of that?

> I hate all those rules! Who cares? Either the relationship is open or it's not.

> We have no rules. If we did, it would put restrictions on each other and we don't want to do that. I want to support Clay in whatever he wants to do. Even if Clay were to meet someone else, I would want the best for him and would support him.

Emergent rules

15% of couples had fluid, emergent rules. In general, they hadn't talked through norms and had no set guidelines. This left them with a general fuzziness about what exactly might be okay, but within the context of "we're pretty relaxed about all this". For example, what to disclose after going out might be ambiguous. "Sometimes I share and sometimes I don't - it depends on the situation."

Although things are left rather loose, a rule might emerge in response to a particular situation or problem. An example might be requiring a partner to stop seeing someone with whom he was getting too involved.

> For the first couple of years there was an assumption of monogamy – at least I had an assumption we would be monogamous. What was clear is that we would be completely honest with each other and we did that. There were occasional 'outside sex' exceptions and then we would talk about it. It was difficult and some of it was painful. I often got very emotional. I especially got angry when I found out Thierry had had sex with a former boyfriend. Rationally, I thought it was okay, but emotionally, it hurt. After a number of these experiences, we came to our first rule: "To talk about it ahead of time".

Spoken & unspoken norms

43% of couples had at least a few norms – patterned behavior that provided a framework from which to operate. Although they may never have explicitly agreed on a specific rule, they described shared understandings and jointly held values that strongly influenced their thinking and behavior.

We don't really have defined rules. We do have the norm of playing together. We played apart some early on, but we realized we'd rather keep it inside. We shifted to playing together about a year into the relationship. We want to keep our sex drive in the relationship. It's not a rule, but I think we have a shared understanding about playing together and what's priority.

There are no rules or restrictions around emotional involvement, but there is concern. We both love each other and we know since we're not having sex with each other, there is a potential to fall in love. I did meet someone I fell in love with. I certainly wasn't going to pack up, but I got very emotionally involved. I've learned to pay attention.

Our basic policy is to try and play together. It's okay if something presents itself when you're on your own, but we don't put much energy there. It has to be respectful. It's not okay to suck everything in sight and it's not okay to leave the other person sitting at home while you go cruise. It's not really rules-based, but we have a pretty good understanding.

We don't have set rules around it, but we choose not to have affairs. You can see the flags go up when someone is getting emotionally involved, and we pull ourselves back. The agreement is: be careful; don't get too involved and jeopardize the relationship.

We don't really have rules, but we both realize that we're dedicated to each other. It's been an understanding that's developed. If something happens (individual sex), eventually, we will talk about it. At first it was kind of scary, but then we got over it. It's just sex. The first fear was one of us would get emotionally attached, but now we realize our emotional attachment is to each other only. We have fuck buddies, but we don't see them outside of a sexual context. They don't become social friends. For us, that would signify an emotional attachment.

Clear rules

32% of couples had rules and found them helpful for guiding behavior, reassuring one another and building a greater foundation of trust.

We set down some rules when we first agreed:

- If we go out together; we come home together
- If we go out together and one wants to go off or stay out longer, we want to know where he is going and what to expect.
- We enjoy each other, but if something comes along – we take advantage.
- We only do 3-ways if we both agree on the person.
- We talk about if it we've done something – always above board
- If one of us is on holiday, it's okay to have outside sex (partner is back home).

We have the same norms we began with. Nothing has changed

- No anal intercourse with outsiders (it's our way of protecting ourselves from a health perspective)
- Only go out when one is traveling or out of town
- If we're together, we play together. Although we do go to the sauna together, and sometimes play separately while we're both there.
- Not allowed to see someone more than once.
- If you arrange to meet that same person again, that's not okay – that's an affair. No planning.

Our spoken rules: When we go out together, we come home together. We tend to stick pretty close to each other. Whether at the baths or a party, we can go off for a little while, but then check back. We touch base a lot.

Our unspoken rules: When we travel, it's okay to fool around (either of us). We don't need to tell or inform the other unless it's extremely hot, tragic, or silly.

Setting the rules ahead of time in terms of what we would and would not do was very important. For example, neither of us will get fucked. We feel that part of our relationship is a 'sacred thing' that we only want to do with each other.

The rules change

Although some couples stay consistent with their initial rules, many find the rules evolve as they discover first-hand what works, doesn't work, and what's actually needed:

Sean

We originally started with a bunch of rules. No one can spend the night. Nobody more than twice. That lasted about a year and then one day I came home and Chuck asked me about a guy he met online. It was my ex-boyfriend. We invited him for the weekend and had a great time. He still comes and stays with us a couple times a year and is a good friend. It's okay to play separately, but we put most of our energy into three-ways. We have a number of friendships that are sexual with the two of us, but not separately. We only play without the other when it just happens at the gym or traveling. We don't develop friendships without the other.

Chuck

Our initial rules evolved. Now we don't always play together, but most of the time. It's okay to do someone multiple times. We have friends with benefits and we've often had guys come and visit and stay with us for the weekend. The rule around that is they sleep in the guest room. Things are pretty fluid. If we're both attracted to someone, than that person has to want to play with both of us.

Stewart

We have pretty clear rules, although they're evolving:

- Twice is the limit to see any particular person, although Lee found guys he liked playing with that I met and didn't feel were a threat and so we began allowing fuckbuddies.

- The overnight rule has evolved to its okay when you're out of town.

- The anal sex rule has remained, but I would very much like to change it. Lee's not into anal sex, but I'm getting increasingly into it. It's getting harder for me not to do it. Tricks will say, "But no one will ever know." But of course, I would know. We talk about it periodically.

Lee

- We always tell each other, including the details.

- I always tell whoever I am playing with that I am partnered and I will be telling him.

- We have to play safe. This means no marks, which is a big concession for me.

- Emotional connection is strong because of S/M. The two-time rule saves me. The two-time rule doesn't apply when traveling and it also includes grey for fuck buddies. I have several buddies that I've become friends with. Stewart has met them and isn't threatened by them and they have been integrated into our lives. Stewart doesn't mind if I play with them more than once.

Or fall away

Some couples who start with rules evolve to a place where they are comfortable without them. Over time, they develop a good idea of what to expect, a deeper trust in their partner, and a confidence that they will be able to address issues on a case-by-case basis. The rules may no longer be necessary because both partners are following the spirit behind the rules.

> At first, Jack hardly played out at all, but he did make a bunch of rules for me to play by. But over the years, we relaxed them all. The only rule left is that there be no overnight stays. However, it's okay to spend the night at a trick's, if the other person is out of town. Ironically, now, Jack is the only one going out.

> There are no rules now. But we act based on our feelings for each other. We act respectfully – appreciate each other's needs. We won't do things we know might be hurtful, e.g. dating someone or getting emotionally involved. I want him to be happy and do whatever he needs to be happy.

Typical Rules & Norms

Each couple has to develop and customize their own approach to non-monogamy. Norms were often where couples were the most creative. Injunctions are typically serious and impersonal but given we're gay men, negotiated agreements often had a playful edge or matter-of-fact bluntness. Before sharing the most typical rules, we'd like to share some of the less common rules that joyfully reflect our gay sensibilities.

Ms. Manners' Top Ten List

10. You can see him as many times as you want, but you can't schedule it

9. If they're in our bed when I get home, they're fair game

8. If you're in love with the guy, you're not allowed to fuck with him one-on-one

7. You can put him in the sling, but no cuddling

6. If you bring him home and he's cute, you have to let me join

5. You can fuck whoever you want, but you can't take him to dinner

4. If you're in the mood to fuck someone else, but I'm horny, you have to do me first

3. You have to spend twice as much time with me than with any of your tricks

2. You're only allowed to date the terminally ill

1. "The Sauna Clause": Sex at the gym doesn't count as sex

Honesty

There were a few very prevalent norms. One was the limiting of emotional involvement, which we discussed previously. Even more prevalent was the norm of Honesty – being straightforward with the truth. Whether or not it was explicitly stated, it was apparent in couples' responses and stories. Often it was mentioned as something that didn't exist in a previous relationship. Even couples that preferred not to share much information, usually had a norm of having to respond truthfully and sufficiently to a partner's questions. Honesty was viewed as foundational.

Straight away, I just wanted honesty and I never had it before. Dean's always been honest. Sometimes I don't like what he has to tell me, but he always tells me. I had a boyfriend for 18 years who lied and cheated. He was gorgeous and men were all over him and he would pretend nothing was happening.

We meet people when we're out at parties so another rule is you have to introduce them to me before you leave. That way they clearly know Van has a partner, he has a face and they recognize they are getting permission. This has been valuable because it actually bothers some guys and those are the ones that need to fully recognize that we are partnered. It also gives a clear message that we are being straightforward and that we have agreed upon rules.

Courtesy and consideration

54% of couples with norms mentioned courtesy and consideration. Some couples instinctively practiced this; some had rules that reinforced it.

We're also very considerate. We can be out and if one of us meets someone and the other isn't interested or doesn't find them attractive, it's fine to go home with them. But if we were to meet someone that we both found very attractive, it would be rude for one of us to leave with that person. We make sure that neither of us is going to be hurt.

Courtesy and respect are important. We plan outside sex for times when we're not together. Whatever we want to do together is first priority. If I've played with someone, they need to be courteous to Richard. One guy told Richard he was going to take me away from him and Richard certainly didn't have to tell me not to see him again.

Although we don't have rules, we do have a norm around loyalty. When we're out together, we won't ever leave with someone else or give up any evening to be with a trick, when we could be together. It's partly courtesy, but neither of us would want to do anything that would hurt the other's feelings.

Jose had to learn how to be honest with me and how to remember to keep me in consideration when he did things. There are some unspoken norms now. You have to take me into account. You have to be considerate of my feelings and how it will impact me.

We give each other first choice of time – the right of refusal for any reason. We prefer to spend time together. The right of first refusal? if you're in the mood to fuck someone else, but I'm horny, do it with me first.

We generally try to be courteous and that can be difficult logistically. If I make arrangements to meet someone and then Dallas doesn't have plans and he doesn't have anything to do, I will usually cancel. I would feel guilty. We don't just take off to go have outside sex when we're spending the afternoon together. We try to keep it out of each other's face.

3-way etiquette

Courtesy and consideration were even more carefully cultivated when couples played together with outsiders. Couples had various rules or understandings that ensured each partner felt valued, comfortable and respected.

We both have to feel comfortable. Either one can call the night. We always check. If Ted stops, I can continue, providing he's comfortable. I never want to have sex if it might make Ted uncomfortable or would hurt him in any way. I value Ted and our relationship much more than the pleasures of sex. If Ted isn't turned on to the guy, but I am and I'm getting revved up, I have to throttle down, which is uncomfortable, but I have no problem calling it off and walking away.

We're both there whenever we have outside sex and no one does anyone or anything they don't want to do. We attend events together. If one wants to leave, then we would both leave. If something is happening and I can't get past it, then I would or could say, "Let's stop." But usually we enjoy watching each other. We're both insecure individually, but together we're confident.

Be aware of the other person's feelings, especially if a 3way. If the differences (older/younger; thinner/stockier) get in the way then it's just not going to work. We just do without, rather than have a conflict.

We go out as a team. It seems natural that some people will like one of us; some will like the other. We are very comfortable with watching the other play. Sometimes I will handcuff Jim to a chair and watch others play with him. I love to see him 'go for it.'

Sometimes a person is more attracted to one of us than the other. There are times when Raul really enjoys watching, but we keep track of the other. He will give me a hard pinch and look toward the door if he wants to quit.

Safe sex

43% of couples had rules about safe sex. Some used condoms, some sero-sorted, and some restricted specific behaviors.

Not surprisingly, couples that were HIV negative were more likely to have rules, restrictions, and stronger concerns related to HIV. Of the couples restricting behavior, receptive anal sex was most commonly off limits. A smaller number avoided anal sex altogether and two couples disallowed giving blow jobs.

> We're both negative and want to stay that way. I'm not going to take the risk or break the rule EVER. I've been very cautious since I came out because HIV was already an issue. Health and emotions – we're saving ourselves for each other.

> Sean's concerns are all around health and HIV. We're both HIV negative, but we don't have the same intellectual agreement about HIV transmission, which is the basis for all our rules.

We asked the study participants that had anal sex, about the frequency with which they used condoms.

Predictably, couples that were sero-discordant were more likely to use condoms with each other. Couples where partners were both positive or both negative typically did not use condoms.

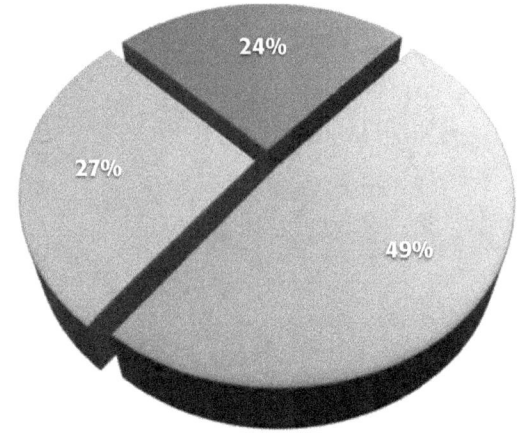

STUDY COUPLES'S HIV STATUS

24% - both HIV positive
49% - both HIV negative
27% - mixed antibody status

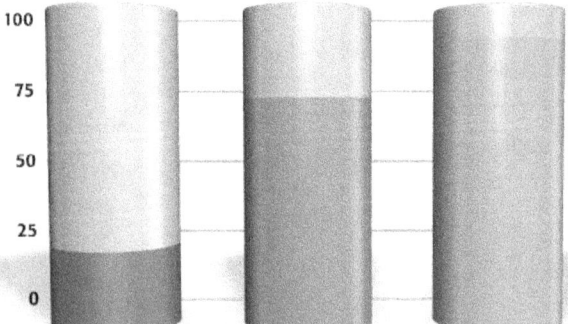

PARTICPANTS' SAFE SEX PRACTICES

25.3% - frequency participants used condoms **with partner**

71.8% - frequency participants used condoms **with outsider of similar status**

89.7% - frequency participants used condoms **with outsider of opposite status**

Other commonly mentioned norms

Below is a list of other commonly mentioned norms. All are attempts to either:

- limit connection or emotional involvement

- prevent discomfort, hurt feelings, and jealousy; or

- ensure partners practice safe sex

Other Commonly Mentioned Norms
32% - Can't bring them home
22% - Can't stay out all night
20% - Veto rights – We stop if I'm uncomfortable
16% - Can't go home with them
11% - Can't see them more than once (or twice)
11% - Restrictions on specific sex acts, e.g. "No receptive anal sex"
11% - Okay to play when out of town

A norm we recommend

We conclude this segment with one norm that we heard from several couples that made good sense to us:

If things aren't going well between us, it's not a good time to play outside the relationship. I've put off guys, when John and I are having trouble.

There have been a few times when we were going through rough times in the relationship and we made a point not to go out during those times.

Primary commitment has always been clear and is even clearer now. Bottom line is: "What's my core commitment?" If we were ever in a place where that was in question or we were having trouble as a couple, that would be a time not to go out. If we were having problems, we shouldn't being going outside, we should be home tending the relationship.

Challenges and Difficulties

We asked participants what they felt was difficult or most challenging about non-monogamy. The top response was Jealousy.

	What Is Most Difficult?
21%	Jealousy
20%	One or both getting too emotionally involved
12%	Becoming comfortable with Non-Monogamy
11%	Challenges that arise in 3-ways
9%	Dishonesty
8%	Issues related to Drug/Alcohol Use
7%	Lack of sensitivity
20%	"Nothing has been difficult"

Jealousy

21% of participants said jealousy was a difficulty or had been a difficulty at some point. Based on the research and articles about non-monogamy, we would have expected this number to be higher. Furthermore, many of the participants who mentioned jealousy talked about it as something they had gotten past. However, for some, particularly partners who were competitive, jealousy definitely was a source of tension.

I can be extremely jealous. Jay tells me what he's done right away, but I have a hard time listening to it. Sometimes I say, "That's enough. I don't want to hear any details." I get really competitive with guys I know that have done him. I compare myself to them and wonder if they're better sex than me. Interestingly, I don't get jealous when we do three-ways. I love to see him having a good time. I love to see two guys having at him and sometimes I may just watch, although usually not. When I see him enjoying himself and having so much fun, I know that's what I want. I guess it over-rides any competitive feelings – I just don't go there.

Initially it would bother me to see Brent kissing another man. We talked about it and he quickly agreed not to. But over time it became okay with me.

Occasionally I get jealous when I'm not included. I tell Barrett when it happens and he's good about hearing me and reassuring me.

He attracts tricks better than me. He's younger. Sometimes feelings of jealousy come up. I have a pang of jealousy when he's been with someone hotter than me and I know he's been getting fucked by someone that he's hot for. But I don't like to hang onto negative emotions. I don't like to let them spiral out of control. I figure it out on my own and drown the feeling with the reminder of how great our relationship is.

Jack

At one point, I set Miles up with a trick I knew he was really hot for. When Miles came back, he went on and on about how wonderful the guy was and I got really jealous. We've learned to share what happened without the enthusiasm, out of respect for the other partner. We both can get jealous and feel insecure at times. It also happens if someone pays attention to one of us more than the other. Not feeling equal is a big trigger. And it was hard sometimes to see Miles getting fucked by someone when it seemed like he was enjoying it more than he did with me.

Miles

Jealousy has been the hardest issue. If one of us had 'too good' of a time or 'gushed' about it, then the other one would get jealous and feel inadequate or insecure. When jealousy comes up, we just talk through it. We don't fight about anything else, so we try to listen to each other and work it out or take it to therapy.

Jealousy - Fear of losing partner

Jealousy is often triggered by the fear of losing out to a rival. 14% mentioned fear of losing their partner to someone else as something they had felt at some point.

I used to get insecure and worry that Ross would find someone else more attractive and leave me. It's not really an issue now. At the Baths, I love to see Ross get sucked off in the steam room - it doesn't make me jealous at all.

Jealousy has been hard. I'm the one that gets jealous – it's usually if I see him with someone I think is cute. It's not a competitive jealousy. It's more that I begin to worry where I stand with David. At this point, I realize it isn't likely (to lose David) and I reassure myself. If it really bothers me, I bring it up. David is reassuring. He reminds me it's just sex – it's nothing to do with emotional ties. It's a lot less now. I'd say it was a 10 and now it's a 3.

I was more interested in other guys than Lewis was and he had this fear that I was going to leave him. Ironically, I think being able to include others took care of my needs such that Lewis is less concerned about me leaving now.

Kurt

The frequency has been hard. Paul goes to the baths 2-3 times a month. That seems like a lot to me. I really don't understand Paul's interest in the baths and outside sex. Paul has reassured me that he has no intention of falling in love and replacing me. I still need to hear that he won't find 'the new Mr. Right.'

Paul

The most difficult thing was physically leaving to go to the baths for the first time, knowing that Kurt was at home and unhappy about it. I knew I had to do it in order to be happy but I had to convince Kurt that it wasn't about him. No one could be everything I want.

Jealousy - Envy

Whereas jealousy is about something one has and is afraid of losing, envy refers to wanting what the other one has (or preventing them from having it). 6% of participants mentioned envy or experiences of envy.

He's hooking up with more guys than me. I'm not jealous. I'm just envious that he's getting it and I'm not. I realize with time, it balances out, but it's my own insecurity.

At times I would feel envious - he's getting it; he's attractive; he's alive and I'm not.

Jealousy - Insecurity

Jealousy, fear, and envy (and sometimes anger) can get jumbled together. Often the underlying emotion is hurt (My self-worth or position has been injured) or insecurity (I have doubts about my position or self-worth). The emotional reaction may be triggered by the other person's actions, but is rooted in one's own sense of security and self-esteem.

Feeling insecure was hard. It helped me appreciate my first partner's insecurity.

Dealing with insecurity. It's more my issue. People are attracted to Rick because he's older, bigger and has a big dick. It's important to remember that Rick loves me enough that he wouldn't leave me.

Feeling left out and feeling fearful and jealous. It's only been intermittent, but there were definitely times.

Because I'm older, sometimes when we go out together, people will look at him before they look at me (he's younger and he's better looking than me). So at the sauna, I just let him go do whoever. It doesn't bother me. He's younger and more buff.

Pat gets jealous. He doesn't understand why I don't. I tell him it's because I trust him. I only want Pat here if he wants to be here. I tell him if he stops loving me, he should move on. I'm secure about who I am and I feel secure in the relationship. I was really sick in the hospital and almost died and Pat was there for me. I know he really loves me.

For Jack, "It's just sex." He says it's meaningless, but I feel hurt and insecure when he goes out. It really affects my self-esteem. I don't think relationships have to be monogamous, but I do think sex is an important aspect of the relationship and I don't take it lightly.

Dale

Sometimes it's still hard. I can feel hurt, angry, jealous, envious. It was hard for Chuck because he knew I would have this big emotional reaction and he knows I could be happy being monogamous. I try to understand my reactions and look at how much of it is about self-esteem. I focus on things that make me feel good about myself like my job, my art. It's more to do with how I'm feeling about myself than who or what Chuck does. It's definitely easier if I've been playing around myself. Sometimes I do that prophylactic ally - preventive medicine.

Chuck

The hardest thing for me is knowing that it sometimes hurts Dale when I go out. We changed our 'honesty rule' to 'we only have to tell when asked'. That's been helpful. I think it's hardest for Dale when I go out when he isn't feeling particularly good about himself. But I still go out.

Jealousy - Antidotes

Interestingly, many brought jealousy up as something they had learned to conquer or keep at bay. Feeling secure seemed to be an antidote. To get there, participants talked about reassurance, building self-esteem, focusing on what they have, and/or feeling generous toward their partner.

Sometimes when they were very attractive, I would be thinking 'Is he a threat to me?' Knowing the fact that he was coming home with me – I reassured myself

---

It took a lot of self-acceptance and letting go of my insecurities. When I accepted Ron, then I had to look at myself – all the reasons I felt I wasn't good enough, not cute enough, don't have enough hair, not good enough at sex, too heavy. And I came to terms with who I am and where I found value in myself. This has been really important for me.

It helps me to understand my own feelings, where they come from, and how they affect me - but not allow my feelings to take over and control my life. I can recognize I'm feeling angry or jealous, but then I think, "Okay. Enough of this shit. Get over it". I value my relationship and I focus there.

When I get jealous, we back off from going out for awhile until we're both ready to do it again. I remember that at a very deep level I know we're not going to break up, and I also remind myself it's not that big of an issue.

I worry about STDs, but I don't get jealous.. I like that I don't feel the need to 'own' Steven. I believe that you have to to want to be together and that people will only stick around if they want to. I don't believe in 'trapping' each other. I don't compete with the guys Steven has sex with – I am who I am and I'm comfortable with that.

Ed was very different from my first love – we're much more honest and grown-up. Sometimes I had trouble knowing what I felt or expressing what I felt. It could be me getting close to someone or Ed getting too close to someone and me feeling hurt. It took a few years to feel more secure. We're quite secure in who we are now. Why? Therapy and practice - realizing it was a different relationship; realizing what I was feeling; remembering I could express it.

My first lover taught me how not to be jealous. We lived in the Castro and he didn't work at an office and he had a notoriously big dick and he was very clear that he wanted an open relationship. I loved this man so much I decided I couldn't deny this love because of jealousy. I discovered I could have a relationship and have a lot of sex with a lot of other people."

I occasionally get jealous around Jerry and I've learned to take that as a signal I need more time with him or reassurance. Jealousy is a very transitory emotion if you don't feed into it.

I feel secure in the relationship. If someone could make him happier through sex & take him away, then we didn't have much going on in the first place."

I just ignore my jealousy. I deal with it and go to sleep and the next day it's gone.

Discomfort with non-monogamy

12% of participants described difficulties becoming comfortable with non-monogamy or the decision to open the relationship. Some participants described initial discussions as what was most difficult. Some spoke of internal conflicts about being non-monogamous. Some reported that openly sharing information and expressing feelings was difficult. And a few reported that their differences about opening the relationship were still unresolved.

Just getting clear at the beginning. It's gotten increasingly comfortable. I don't feel any jealousy.

Talking about it, especially at the beginning. Coming up with the groundrules was hard.

At first, it's getting over the idea of having an open relationship. In my previous relationships, we were never open. However, I got over this. The first couple of times we played alone at a sauna it was a little uncomfortable, but it was easier since we were both in the same location. Otherwise, it's never really caused an issue for us.

There's still a part of me that feels like I'm doing something wrong. I can come home feeling sleazy. It's not about the couple, but a little voice saying "There's no commitment; It's just casual; Is this good for us?"

Being open and communicating and sharing feelings is hard for me. Sometimes I can do it and sometimes Ryan has to guess what I'm feeling and draw it out of me.

Coming to a level of acceptance. I was raised in a charismatic Christian church. Being gay and sex outside of marriage were both wrong. I've had to realize that's not the case for everyone. It's taken work. I had to change my morals, e.g. I had to decide it's okay not to be restricted to one person.

What's still difficult is Ray sometimes gets emotionally upset because I'm going out. He wished I wouldn't or that I would do it less often. He feels hurt by it. On the other hand, he's not all that interested in sex with me when I initiate it. We've had an agreement to be open for 25 years, but it's not resolved. I try to compromise or negotiate. Sometimes he gets upset and sometimes it doesn't bother him.

It feels like being open is a threat to our relationship – it's definitely a source of tension. Right now I feel guilty because he's not going out much so does that mean he's more invested in the relationship than I am? It's a question of weighing the needs of each individual with the needs of the relationship.

Connor

I spend an undue amount of time thinking about it and worrying about it. I spend lots of time on the computer trying to hook up and planning it so it won't be in Logan's face. Logan thought we needed to break up. We went to a counselor for 5 sessions and worked through some of the issues.

We eventually agreed to have an open relationship. However, we are still working out the rules.

Logan

I recognize and remember the good things we have. It's way too much to throw out. I chose not to leave the relationship even though Connor is strongly committed to continuing to go out. Of course, it would have been better if we had firm agreements on the front-end.

The challenges of 3-ways

11% of participants reported difficulties when playing as a couple with outsiders. Finding the outsider can be challenging and how the outsider relates to both partners can trigger many of the same feelings of jealousy and insecurity mentioned previously. Some couples avoid playing together for this reason; others become skilled at paying close attention to these dynamics.

We soon realized that we needed to play separately. Being a mixed race couple made it difficult to do three-ways. People weren't attracted to me or sometimes they would only be attracted to me. Stan is more outgoing and people find that attractive. He would bring them in, but often they would only be interested in him. I was treated poorly. I had to come to terms with it and realize it was their problem – but it meant playing separately. Stan didn't realize the disconnect because he was into the moment of relating to them. It wasn't that he was insensitive, but he was oblivious and I had to make him aware. On rare opportunities we find someone who is attracted to both of us and we can play together. It's a real treat. There's more of a connectedness with that person and we can share the experience together.

Learning to make sure everyone is involved. Once in Amsterdam, we were doing a 3-way and I noticed Wayne stepped outside. I went outside and he explained that he felt left out and it was okay for me to continue. I told him we started together and we will finish together and brought him back in. I reassured him and I've learned to pay attention to how involved everyone feels.

We have such different types that it was really difficult when we only played together. We've also had issues when the third liked one of us more than the other. They don't need to like us both equally, but they have to be respectful and join with both of us.

It's hard to find guys we're both sexually compatible with. A lot of guys don't like 3-ways and it might be easier to just play independently. We've discussed it, but we don't want to dissipate our sexual energy elsewhere. We're still sexual together and like to spend a lot of time together.

Dishonesty

9% of participants mentioned a point in their relationship when they, their partner, or the two of them were not being fully forthright about their outside sex. Examples included covert outside sex prior to opening the relationship (discussed previously), illicit affairs (most of which eventually surfaced), not abiding to agreed upon rules, and partners used to habitual outside sex having trouble fully disclosing.

Initially, I played around and then lied about it. It really takes a long time to regain the trust of your partner after you've lied.

Les not being honest with me early on was very difficult. As trust with each other grows, we understand each other better, although it's been hard.

After we opened it up, Skip began to break the rules – on numerous occasions. We still have rules, although I'm not sure Skip always follows them.

Drug/Alcohol issues

8% of respondents mentioned difficulties with drug use related to outside sex. In most cases, crystal (meth-amphetamine) cocaine and alcohol were the drugs that were problematic. Most of the participants that brought this up were at least several years into abstinence and/or recovery. They reported heavy drug use in previous periods of their lives, difficulties with others who were heavy users, and/or the prevalence of unsafe sex when high. A few participants acknowledged current drug use and their on-going need to curtail or manage this when being sexual.

Early on, it was insecurity around the relationship. If its once every few months – no problem, but there was a period when Taylor was doing crystal meth and having a lot of outside sex. It was a big deal. I finally told him it was rehab or the end of the relationship. He went into a program and has never slipped in the last 6 years.

We had to end the relationship with the guy when it became apparent that he wouldn't do anything without being high – not even see a movie.

We were partying and having group sex when we met. We were seriously involved with crystal and crack, but soon after we met, we both stopped using. Now we depend on each other.

Drugs and alcohol have always been a part of the scene when we played outside. We used condoms about 70% of the time, but the other 30% of the time was terribly unsafe.

I've been in recovery for 8 years, but it still comes up. Sex and drugs used to be synonymous for me – I couldn't do one without the other. I'm still re-claiming sex from 'sex and drugs'.

Lack of sensitivity

7% mentioned their partner's insensitivity. It wasn't seen as intentional, but more a general lack of awareness – a pattern of being so focused on their own concerns and pleasure, they forget to track or take into account the impact an action might have on their partner. In most cases, although the partner learned to be more aware and less insensitive, it continues as an on-going issue rearing its head periodically.

I'm pretty aware of Xavier. If anything I do might hurt him, I will stop. I think Xavier is less sensitive. He lives in the moment much more than I do.

Initially Tom saw everything through his own lens and didn't include me in the equation when he made decisions. He's learning to take my feelings into account.

When Tim got too involved, I had to let him know it hurt me. He's more emotionally available than me and so it's hard for him to compartmentalize sex. But I'm more self-aware. I can tell when something isn't the right thing to do. I may do it anyway, but it won't even occur to Tim that something isn't the right thing to do.

Other responses

Two other responses to the question about difficulties were common. 20% mentioned one or both partners getting too emotionally involved. We addressed this previously in the section on Connection and Involvement.

For another 20%, the response was: "Nothing. It's never been a problem."

> Nothing has been too hard. I'd say not being explicitly open for all those years was the most difficult thing. I always wanted to be open sooner.

> Outside sex really hasn't been difficult. The biggest issue is trying to spice up our own sex life and keep it active.

> We've never had a big fight about the issue. We may have had disagreements about the timing, but opening the relationship hasn't been a big source of tension.

What Helps

We asked couples what helped make non-monogamy work for them. Many participants gave a comprehensive list of factors. Below are a few representative lists followed by the key themes we heard about What Helps:

- We're easy-going and non emotional about outside sex.
- We communicate a lot, which is key. We realize the benefits to the relationship of communicating.
- We use our outside sexual experiences to fuel our own at-home sex.
- We have a high level of trust in each other, but we don't take each other for granted.

- Having a clear understanding of the arrangement takes away the difficulties.
- We make a clear distinction between emotional and physical needs.
- We constructively talk about the issues when we need to.
- We're both physically driven men (sexually), but we're both solidly committed to the emotional aspects of our relationship. We're on the same page on this.

- Discussing it openly.
- Establishing a firm foundation of trust
- Taking it slowly
- We know we always want to be together
- We recognize and differentiate between sex and love
- We developed clear norms that we could follow

What Helps:

65%	Communicating Openly and Honestly	18%	Learning to deal with Jealousy – Building Self-Esteem
65%	Being Truthful/Honest	18%	Getting Support from Therapists or Mentors
52%	Trusting (each other and the relationship)	17%	Setting Groundrules
34%	Reassurance & Appreciation	6%	Practicing Moderation
30%	Respecting Partner and their differences		

Communicating openly and honestly

The most common response was honest, open communication. 65% included this in their response to the question about what helps.

Communication! Honesty! Openness! The more we talk the better we feel. Knowing there are no surprises or secrets makes it much easier. I would have big problems if I didn't know who or what Elliot was doing outside the relationship.

Talking about it and being honest. If there's a problem, surface it, rather than gunny sacking it. If you can talk about this, it makes talking about other issues that much easier. It's really important to talk honestly, why you want to have outside sex, what it means to you, and then jointly decide the parameters.

The ability to communicate effectively. We can get pissy and childish, but then we pull back and work it out. One of our great strengths is we have the ability to talk openly about potentially difficult things without getting dramatic. We hear each other's concerns and sometimes we have to put it aside and come back when we're calmer, but we always come back and resolve it. In previous relationships, those fractures never got healed. We're able to resolve things and move on.

It's important to me that we've stayed connected and in good communication with each other about outside sex. We have grown together in this area rather than grown separately. This has allowed us to incorporate outside sex in a healthy way.

We're honest about everything, even if it bothers the other person. We didn't used to communicate well. We would argue about doing the dishes, when that wasn't the real issue.

After 15 years, there's a lot more understanding: "Oh, it's your back that's hurting; it's not about me." It's painful for me to not talk and it's painful for Allen to talk. So we've had to learn how to talk while trying not to overdo it. We've learned how to communicate. And when I get really pissed, I have to remember how much I love him.

You have to talk it through. Nothing is off the table - being straightforward and trustful and honest even if your first impulse is fear or shame.

We learned how to communicate with each other 17 years ago. We were both from highly dysfunctional families, but we learned from our 12-step programs how to communicate. We have a common language.

Being able to talk things out. I will tell Dean if I feel he's falling in love with someone. If it's serious, Dean will figure it out. And Dean sees my patterns and knows what's going on. He helps me through these situations.

Frequency of relationship discussions

We also asked couples to rate the frequency with which they discussed relationship issues (regardless of topic). Below are participants' responses. A few observations:

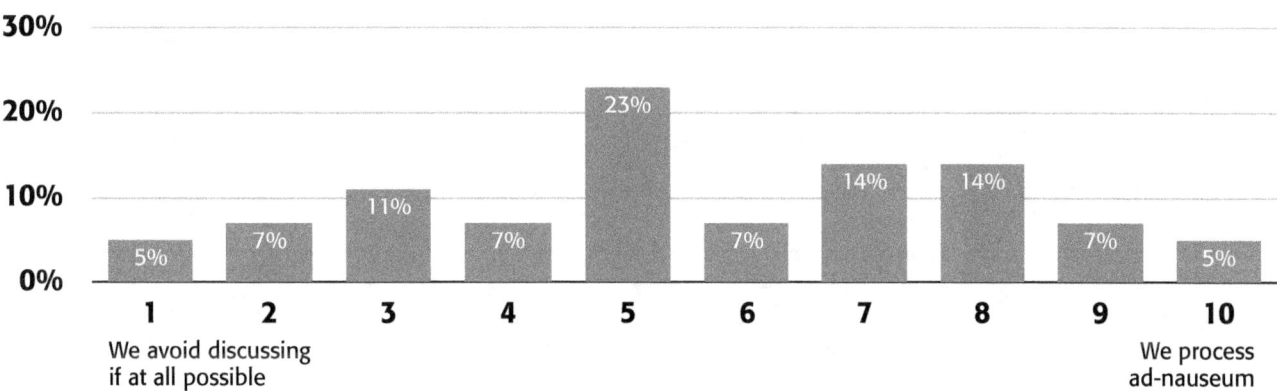

- Couples scoring lower often commented "We don't have many issues".
- Couples scoring lower tended be the ones that disclosed less about outside sex.
- Couples scoring higher were more comfortable with difficult conversations, more likely to form connections with outsiders and enjoyed sharing their internal experience
- Most of the '1' scores were only one partner – not both, and often indicated concern – "We don't talk enough."
- Approximately 20% of the couples had strong differences where one partner preferred relationship discussions more than the other. This could be a source of friction, but most commented on how they had found a middle ground.

Being truthful/honest

Honesty was often linked with comments about communication, but it was also mentioned separately, in its own right. 65% spoke about the importance of being truthful.

Being honest. The more I was honest, the less problems we had.

We've done a really good job of being honest and being honest about our emotions. You have to be honest to make it work, given our rules. It's the whole continuum from "Who do you find attractive?" to "I'm feeling very emotionally involved and don't want to stop seeing him." Being that honest has helped build trust in the foundation of our relationship.

We're totally honest and that has really helped. We lay out the 'warts and all' for each other to see.

Honesty is the most important. Not just saying everything, but understanding the other person's feelings and concerns and sharing things in a considerate manner. Knowing that I will have to tell Walt, keeps me from doing certain things. I know whatever I do, I will have to tell him, so it helps me draw the boundary. It helps me avoid unsafe sex or doing someone he wouldn't approve of in a public place.

We both had prior relationships where partners cheated. Neither of us wanted that again. We've always been open and honest with each other for that reason.

The thing that supported us and was bedrock was our agreement about mutual honesty. I knew I would tell him and I knew he would tell me, no matter how uncomfortable it was going to make either of us.

Trust

52% of participants named 'Trust' in response to the question "What helps?" Trust, which is an important ingredient in any relationship seems pivotal in a non-monogamous relationship. Participants talked about trust as both an action and an outcome. An active belief in their partner's love and integrity reassured them when they might be feeling fearful or insecure.

I trust that Pete wouldn't go out on me. I trust him 100%.

I trust in the 'concern for the other'. I trust Bill is deeply concerned about my happiness.

We have an absolute trust in each other and in our relationship. We trust that we can work out any issues that come up.

You have to build trust in a relationship and ultimately you have to let go. You can't be insecure really or jealous or it won't work. I experienced all that early on, but it's all about building trust. Yes, there's a danger that the relationship could end, but if you want to have the ability to go out, then you have to learn to trust the other person. It takes time and a certain commitment to the relationship.

There's always going to be something else with this issue. Its trial and error and you have to push the boundaries occasionally and trust that if it becomes a problem we will work it out and self-correct. Trust that it won't jeopardize the on-going relationship and the intention for it to continue.

Trust as an outcome

Trust as an outcome was built through consistent love, caring and commitment. If partners were consistently honest with each other, trust deepened. We heard repeatedly from couples, as their experience of successfully trusting each other grew, it became easier to manage the ambiguity of an open relationship.

The two times I got too involved, I stopped because Paul told me I had to. That actually increased the trust in the relationship because now he knew I would stop if he asked and I became more aware and committed to paying attention. The depth of our trust wouldn't be possible without having gone through that test. We've learned to respect each other's concerns.

Opening up the relationship has been a hurdle, but once you work your way through it, you know you can work through anything and the trust factor goes up tenfold.

Although it was easy to come to agreement, being open from the beginning made it tougher to build the relationship. There wasn't a deep foundation of trust to rely on. We had to get comfortable telling the other person what we had done and we had to get comfortable hearing it. But this allowed the trust to happen and the foundation to develop.

We were sure we would stay together, so that helped because we didn't worry about that. That probably fell in place after about 10 years of being together.

It's allowed us to be more trusting of each other. You always know at the end of the day that the other person will be at home there for you. They aren't going anywhere. It's actually made our relationship stronger.

We're probably more stable because of the struggles around outside sex. It gave us both the opportunity to show the other that we had some restraint. I've had 2 or 3 guys that I was seeing a few times, 'propose' to me. I had to tell them that I must not have made myself completely clear and then ended the connection.

We feel very attuned. I don't feel we will ever break up. We complement each other. Our connection is so strong. I think all this allows us to trust each other.

Appreciation and reassurance

Appreciation of their partner and the relationship was a key support for 34% of participants. The relationship and life created together was reassuring - helping them look past the smaller issues and keep things in perspective. Sometimes individuals needed to be reminded of their partner's love and loyalty, e.g. "I needed to hear that he wouldn't leave me." But often they reminded and reassured themselves.

We've seen a lot of our friends break up and then wished they hadn't. It makes us appreciate what we have and so we give each other a little more space because we know we value each other and our relationship. It helps us trust that we're both going to come home.

We have similar values, a similar sense of integrity. We really appreciate who the other person is.

Focusing on the big picture of the relationship helps. I can't imagine ever being happy with anyone but Phillip. I've never met anyone else that I would want to spend my life with. It puts the outside sex in perspective. I know why outside sex is important to Phillip, but more importantly is why I'm with Phillip and that has allowed outside sex to be relatively easy to deal with.

It probably doesn't get talked about much, but there is the reassurance of time passing. We're still coming home; we still love each other; we're still going about the day-to-day of living our lives together.

The commitment of not ever leaving allowed us to get rid of fear. At year #5, I told Taylor that "I'm in regardless." From that point on, I was no longer going to ever entertain the notion that bailing was an option. It laid a foundation and the fear of talking about difficulties or being completely honest about anything went away.

We realize our relationship is strong at the foundation. The primary commitment has always been clear and is even clearer now.

We always did a great deal together regardless of any problems in this arena and that was helpful. We had a lot else that was good and that fueled our love and trust and commitment.

Respecting partner and their differences

30% of participants named respect as an important helper. Participants spoke of respecting a partner's feelings and sensibilities, but also acknowledging and honoring a partner's differences.

The key for us is we have respect for each other and for each other's feelings. We've stayed committed and we follow our agreements.

I had to really respect what he wants or doesn't want. He has to take time to process and he doesn't like being surprised. He tends to see things in black and white – he knows something is either right or wrong for him. He won't do something he really doesn't want to do. I was pushing the boundaries and so I had to make sure he was comfortable with the changes. If he's insecure or pissed, I will know it and I need to reassure him.

We both have strong personalities and we've adapted to each other. We had to get to a place where it is okay to disagree and realize that neither of us is wrong, we just have different views.

I've seen other couples where one person becomes too tolerant of their partner. It's vital to speak up; to take a stand; "There are certain things I will not allow. There are certain things that are deal-breakers". Examples? Inattention – being emotionally left out; Not being treated as a partner in all ways; Respect.

Both people have to be willing to accept that they are going to grow and change. The reason our relationship works is because we both want the other to grow and experience their dreams. Tony is very secure and doesn't get jealous. Because he's so trusting, it gives me a lot of latitude to explore myself.

Respecting each other's opinions and styles is critical. We make a habit of communicating preferences in the moment and we consider the other person's feelings a lot. We check in, "Are you okay?" - my partner's opinion matters as much as my own.

Getting support

18% of participants talked about getting outside support. This took two forms. Some utilized therapists and counselors (separately or as a couple). Some had friends or mentors that they felt they could confide in and use as a sounding board. The enthusiasm of couples who had mentors was in marked contrast to the couples who complained of feeling isolated and unable to find couples who would talk openly.

Being able to talk with other couples about how they handle the issue helps us normalize. Rather than demonize the outside sex, as we were raised, they were supportive. It helped to hear, "It's not about 'infidelity' or 'cheating' which are derogatory terms; it's about 'play'. Couples counseling has also helped.

We were lucky enough to have mentors. Our friends supported us and talked with us about it. They said, "Our biggest regret was we didn't allow ourselves to explore when we had the most opportunities. We waited until we had overcome our insecurities." We tried to learn from that and not be quite so cautious.

Having mentors was a big help. We knew them for five years. One passed away, but we still have Tom and his new partner. We used them as a sounding board. We could see where we stood in relation to them.

We always knew we really loved each other. I knew Graham was the right guy for me. We weren't sure we were going to make it in the first few years. Our friends certainly didn't think so. But we went to couples counseling because we knew we wanted to make it work together.

Couples counseling allowed us or taught us how to communicate well and that made a huge difference.

We did a couple of sessions with a therapist I was seeing for school. That was helpful. It gave us a foundation and helped us develop communication tools (listening and hearing each other).

Don't overdo it

6% of participants mentioned practicing moderation. A few couples talked about periods where they had overdone it. A few participants intimated they thought their partner went out too frequently and/or was compulsive around sex. None of the study couples had rules about overall frequency, but many had norms about what seemed appropriate.

You need to be with other sex partners, but not 'go crazy.' You need to know when to stop and how to control yourself or you'll ruin your relationship. It goes to respecting your partner.

We use it as a treat when we're out of town. It's a way of having fun, as opposed to being on a constant quest for sex. We see some couples that are constantly on the hunt; they have to have a third in order to have sex with each other.

> I do think that because we're a couple there should be some restraint. Saying 'No' every once in awhile is a way of valuing the relationship. A couple of times, I've brought it up, "Look we have a relationship, at least say 'No' to going out sometimes." Like after he's been away for a weekend and going out and then not going out at home the next weekend, in addition.

> We don't overtly go looking. We enjoy going out with each other and being with each other. If a third person presents themselves and decides they're interested – fine. This is partly about courtesy and partly about keeping the focus on us as couple enjoying the moment.

Other helpers

- Learning to Deal with Jealousy and building self-esteem was mentioned by 18% of participants. (See section on jealousy for examples and discussion).

- Setting Groundrules was mentioned by 17%. (See sections on Approaches to Rules/Norms and Typical Rules for discussion and examples).

Couples' Sex Lives Together

What about couples own sex lives together?

To get a sense of how outside sex fit in with study couples' own sex lives together, we asked each participant to tell us what percent of their sex was with their partner, independent of their partner, with their partner and others.

- For some, independent sex is primary.
- Some have no, or very little independent sex.
- For others it falls somewhere in between

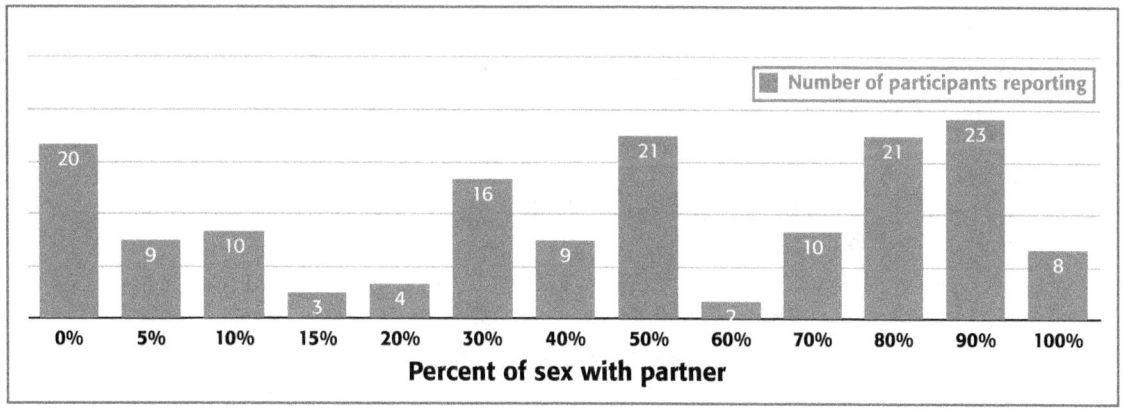

Percent of sex with partner

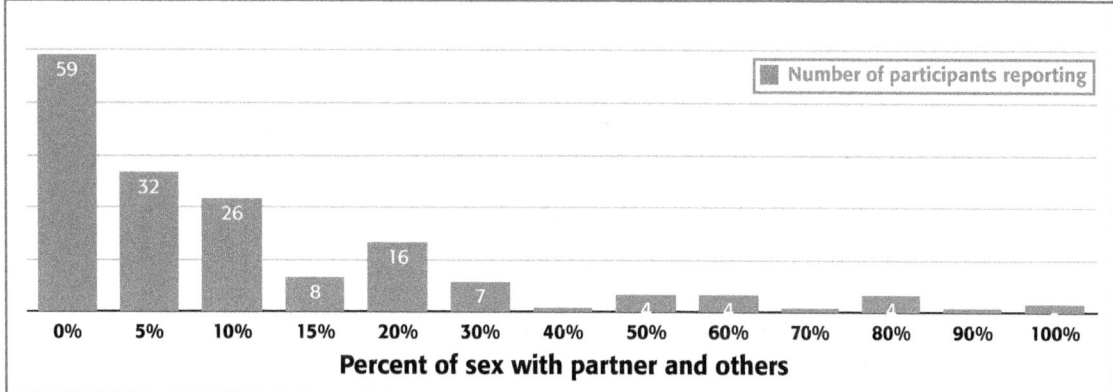

Percent of sex with partner and others

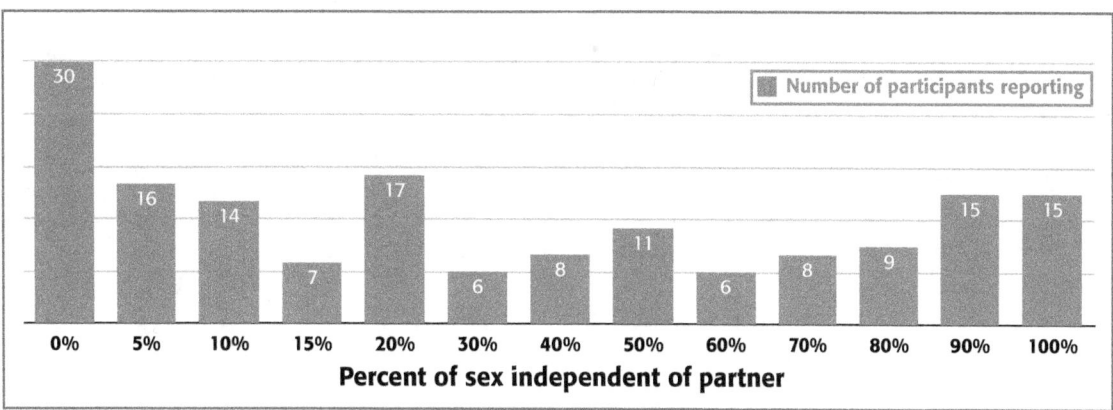

Percent of sex independent of partner

Love without sex

Study couples fell into four clusters in terms of their own sex lives. 15% were couples who no longer had sex together, but still felt very close, loving and connected to each other. One of the biggest learnings for us as authors was to hear couples in this group glowingly talk about their relationship. Prior to the study, we imagined couples whose own sex lives had dwindled were more like room-mates. Repeatedly, we listened to partners talk about their affection and concern for each other, their joy in companionship, their loyalty and commitment. It was quite gratifying to let go of our misperception and we noticed this was the one study finding we most enjoyed sharing when asked what we were learning.

Most of these couples seemed quite comfortable with having let go of their sex lives together. It was shared rather matter of factly – been there, done that and moved on. The 'routineness' of many years with the same person was a leading cause, but some couples acknowledged their early sex lives together had never been terribly passionate or compatible. In other cases, it was more one-sided with one partner having health issues and/or losing interest in sex altogether. A few participants described their own pattern of becoming bored with any partner after a certain amount of time.

Rather than lamenting the lost sex life together, the couples in this cluster focused on the strength and joy in their relationship and were pleased that their open relationship allowed them to carry on as sexual beings without giving up what they most valued. The outside sex for these couples was most often anonymous and characterized as a necessary response to a physical drive. Although it was important not to squelch their sex drive, it was deemed rather insignificant when compared to what they valued in their relationship.

We haven't had much sex together in the last few years, but we're very, very affectionate. We hug, kiss and cuddle all the time. With every encounter, we say we love each other and let the other one know they look great.

Sex is about chemistry. It either works or it doesn't. Our chemistry has been pretty average from the beginning. He's attractive – even more so, now. But he's very vanilla. Outside sex keeps us from wandering. If you can scratch an itch, it feels better, and sometimes that's all it takes. If the sex doesn't work out, do you throw away the rest of the relationship? We threw out the sex and kept the relationship.

Our relationship is now non-sexual, and has been so for 5 years. Our relationship has never really been about sex. Jim would like a bottom, but I don't bottom. And Jim NEVER bottoms, so we're a non-match. We kiss a lot, tell each other we love the other, and hold hands. Outside sex has allowed us to stay together because it isn't a point of contention.

We no longer have sex together. It's been about six years. I'm not a particularly sexual person. I always lose interest and there are many things I'd rather be doing than having sex. I used to worry about what am I not doing right, but I'm comfortable with who I am. We don't have sex, but I don't feel like we've lost anything in the relationship.

I haven't had sex in the last three years with Brad, and not with anyone outside for two years. I don't need outside sex and I have a high level of affection, cuddling, kissing, with Brad that I find very satisfying. He still goes out and I want him to. I don't know if it's physical or emotional, but I just don't have the urge.

I used to feel that things weren't okay with us unless we were having sex. But we have committed to always be together and I trust that. Now, I know it's okay to not be having sex together – our relationship is much more than just sex.

I focus on the good we have. We keep affirming that we love each other and that we want to be together. We don't take each other for granted. When my brother was killed, Allan stepped in and took care of all of us, including my Mom. That's the way he shows me he loves me.

Sex isn't what keeps us together. Sex is a minor thing. I just cherish him and his qualities. He constantly keeps me interested.

What makes us partners if we don't have sex together? In my mind, we're lifetime partners. I can't imagine feeling the way I do about him with anyone else.

On the wane

10% of couples characterized their sex lives as increasingly infrequent or on the wane. Unlike the first group, some of these couples did express a sense of loss, particularly if one partner was still interested (and the other wasn't). Others seemed ambivalent. They wished it was more frequent, but didn't have the energy or the inclination to make it a focus. As with the first cluster, these couples put their emphasis on what they loved and valued about their partner and their relationship.

We don't have as much sex together now, which I would want and we probably go out more. I'm not sure what we can do about that. It changed at some point and we talk about it. We probably aren't working as hard to have sex with each other because we can go out. This isn't the cause of why we're not having that much sex together, but it does lessen the motivation to work on it. Of course, saying we would be monogamous at all costs would be much more negative.

We love each other; we kiss everyday; we snuggle at night. As we age, sex becomes less and less a primary drive. I'm really glad we have everything else together and didn't lose it because of sex.

I am at a place now where I'd much rather have sex with my husband, than anyone else. I don't like the idea of a sexless marriage. It makes me feel old. Love is spiritual. I'm sad that we don't have more drive toward each other.

We just don't fit together sexually. We keep trying. I wish we had it, but it's okay with me that we don't. I wonder if being able to go outside is an easy way out of working on our own sexual intimacy. I hadn't really thought about it until now. But obviously we haven't been very motivated – it may solely be a 'should' from society that we should be having sex together.

We don't have sex. He told me the numbers he gave you and I laughed. I guess he still has some Gloria Vanderbilt notion of what we should be.

We're so much in love with each other, but we know that we have separate sexual interests. We each have guys we trust that we can play with from time to time. But I know what I have in Devon and I really value it. We have the same core values about family, money, interests in people - the things that really matter.

In my last relationship we were monogamous and after 7 years, we had no sex. Having this one be open, I don't have to worry about that happening. As the amount of sex we have together goes down, that won't be a reason for us to break up. It means we will still be able to have outside sex and stay together. It's reassuring.

Fanning the fire

30% of couples were still quite engaged with each other sexually although they expressed concerns about how to keep this alive. Many couples in this group used outside sex to energize their own sex together. Whether by sharing titillating details, experimenting with newly learned techniques, or playing together with outsiders, outside sex was seen as a helpful contributor to keeping their own sex life vibrant. Some couples described having date nights and deliberately setting time aside – making sure it was a priority.

> I didn't want to become roommates. I always kept that in the back of my mind. We got into porn movies; that was stimulating. When I go to The Club, I usually don't get off and so I fuck Barry the next morning. Going out seems to stir things up. We have one couple we play with who never cum with us, but save it for when they go home together.

> We realized we're both still attractive and that makes us more attractive to each other -- we still have something to offer each other. We had become complacent about our sex life. We were always busy with other things and never made the time. We're much more sexual with each other now.

> Terry says he doesn't care how much I get on the outside as long as he's getting some with me. I make a point to make sure he's getting enough. Periodically, I reassess myself. Am I withholding? Am I going outside, instead of having sex with Terry? Is going out tonight good for us?

> I am sometimes regretful that I find it so pleasurable to find sex outside the relationship. I wish we could find all the amusement we needed within the relationship. I don't attach any value to monogamy, so it's not about that. You'd think having the man of my dreams would be enough. We do make date nights. I'm on a medication that affects my erections. If I can't do it, I want him to get his needs met and to feel good. I have no qualms about that. We had a guy give him a superb time – that was hot as all hell for me.

> We both have had previous relationships. We know we have to focus on each other and the relationship. Gene would probably want more sex since his libido is higher than mine. We know we have to take time away from our stress and work-lives and spend quality time. We set up date nights. I also know it's more important to me to have the experience with Gene than alone. I've done the other.

What's Libido Got to Do With It?

We had participants rate their libido on a scale of 1 (low) to 10 (high). The average libido of study participants was 7. We didn't find any important patterns related to libido, but we will share a few observations:

- Our average would be much higher if we included the frequent responses of '11', '12', and 'off the charts' (we scored these as 10's).
- Most participants' libidos were quite similar to the libido of their partner.
- A few participants reported very low libidos, which certainly had an impact on how invested they were in any type of sex. For some, having their partner be able to go out was a relief.
- Although a few commented on their libidos declining as they aged, many participants in their 60's and older reported strong libidos.
- A few related a great deal of fluctuation in their libidos due to steroids, aging or HIV

Still vibrant

The remaining couples (45%) had active sex lives together and a) either made positive comments about this, or b) didn't express concerns. Other than these two criteria, there is no clear distinction between this group and the previous cluster. Couples in both clusters are apt to be 'fanning the fire'.

What's important here is the number of long-term couples that are still quite sexually active with each other. On average, the couples in this cluster had been together 15.3 years, with 6 of these couples having 20+ years together. When combined with the previous cluster, 75% of study couples continued to have active sex lives with each other.

We asked some of the couples who had been together the longest if they had thoughts about what fueled and sustained their sex lives together. Some said sex together had always been a central driving focus. Many related having a fair amount of outside sex with much of it together. Switching roles, high compatibility, a deepening sense of trust, and an appreciation of the ease and intimacy were also offered as contributing factors. A few of these couples noted that their interest in outside sex was waning. Hooking up with others required too much effort and they were finding themselves increasingly content and fulfilled playing at home.

We're both in our 50's and we're becoming insatiable again, but it's mostly with each other. We're closer to monogamy than we were.

It's enhanced our relationship, particularly sexually. We still have sex together after 20 years and it probably wouldn't be as frequent or as passionate. If we were monogamous, we would have bottled up our frustration and I'm 99% sure we'd be doing stuff behind each other's back.

We are more relaxed with each other and we have seen each other in every light possible - seeing all sides of each other. We learned a lot sexually by going out and we added to our sex play together. We've become more appreciative of each other and what we have.

Initially opening the relationship damaged our own sex life. We got excited about the three ways and found that we were saving ourselves for the weekend when we would go out together looking for a third. We weren't having as much sex with each other. I brought it to Mac's attention and said it wasn't okay - we had to put as much energy into our own sex life. We talked about it and made a point to focus on it. At this point, having outside sex has improved our sex life together. We've brought back ideas and techniques and energy and brought it back into the relationship.

Rob

It's made our own sex life better. I don't see how you can stay together and still have a great sex life without having 'outside' inspiration. Your body ages and the libido may vary, so it's a matter of keeping the interest alive. We work to make sex beautiful and interesting. It puts you in a good mindset and makes it something to look forward to. I would really miss it if we stopped.

John:

I find that if things are getting stale, going out together for a 3-some or a party will bring Rob and me closer. I never have a problem with sex; I see it as integral. Rob has ups and downs in terms of his sexual libido. Outside involvement encourages Rob to be more sexual.

What's the Impact? Benefits & Risks

We asked couples to describe the impact outside sex had on their relationship. We were careful to position this question neutrally, without pulling for positives or negatives. If there seemed to be any confusion, we always clarified by saying "we were looking for both positive and negative impact". In the case of participants who had an immediate response of "Nothing has been negative" (end of conversation), we did ask if there had been any positive impact.

Both positive and negative impact

21% of participants shared both positives and negatives in their responses. The quotes below give a perspective of the trade-offs. Notice how many of the benefits go beyond 'just providing a sexual outlet'. And these benefits come with some risk.

✔ Makes relationship more interesting, in general. We're not closed; we're open – so we're meeting new people and that enriches what we bring to the relationship. It forces us to be more honest. It helps us be more willing and comfortable to talk about what might be difficult.

✘ There's people you can't talk to (family and friends) about being non-monogamous. We stopped having sex together a few years ago. Occasionally we do three ways. So that leaves me wondering "Would we have tried harder to make our sex life work together if it were the only option?"

✔ It's created adventure and it's allowed us to join together in playfulness. It encourages us to talk about our feelings and it serves as a catalyst for new perspectives into our relationship. It challenges trust, but on the other hand it helps us hone our sense of trust. If we can navigate it well, we can be more trusting.

✘ In addition to the tension, I worry that it means our relationship is aberrant. There's no clear model and so we don't know if we're doing the right thing or how to do the right thing. And there is stigma to going outside the relationship.

✔ It's helped us evolve. We feel we really want to be together. We've learned that we can trust each other. Ted can go out clubbing and I decided that I could either trust him or not and I realized I clearly trust him. We have better communication because we have talked about outside sex and how to handle it.

✘ The only negative is we have more worries about getting a disease.

✔ It's underscored the importance of honesty in the relationship. It's forced us to be more intentional in how we navigate and evolve the relationship. It's helped increase our communication muscles.

✘ It's brought some pain and confusion and it's required a certain amount of expenditure of energy.

✔ We're probably more relaxed with each other – sex isn't as charged.

✘ It's taken some emphasis off our one-on-one sex. Its spread the focus a little wider and now we're not totally dependent on each other for sex. After a 3-way, sex together is very nice and sometimes it feels less exciting.

✔ It's allowed the relationship to survive. It's brought more honesty and openness to the relationship. We're both reassured about the relationship continuing. We've got several fuck buddies with whom we've become good friends.

✘ There are still moments of jealousy.

✔ It's improved our sex lives both internally (with each other) and externally. We're both more sexually satisfied. It's kept my sex drive going.

✘ The downside is there have been some hurt feelings; I feel distrusted; and there's been a few traumatic situations.

Randy:

✔ I got sexually bored. I also wanted outside validation – "I know Art thinks I'm hot, but I wanted a second opinion." Art also didn't think he was that attractive and so I wanted him to experience that others perceived him similarly to me. He finally opened up to noticing others and their response to him. It was a joy for me to see.

✘ It has introduced something in our relationship that we can't do together. I'm missing him. We also now have 'secrets' from others since we don't tell family and friends.

Art:

✔ I really enjoy the outside sex, so in some ways, it strengthens the relationship. It's a blessing that we can be open so that we can stay together and not be sexually frustrated and biting at each other.

✘ Randy and I are pretty tight emotionally, but being open to outside sex has diminished that a bit. There's a bit of the pie chart missing. There are people outside the relationship with whom we're being intimate and we're not sharing that as it happens. I regret that.

Primarily negative impact

A few participants (4%) shared strong negatives. This was more apt to be the case for couples where the decision to be open or closed is still not fully resolved.

✗ It's brought issues of insensitivity and lack of confidence to the fore. It's allowed me to observe both our behaviors. The issues would be there anyway, but they get exacerbated by sex. We get competitive around sex.

✗ It hasn't always gone well. There have been a lot of hurt feelings and arguments. It's been one of the more difficult aspects of our relationship. However, we both believe that sex is very important. I don't believe any one person can meet all of your sexual needs. So, we keep coming back to outside sex and we're getting better about communicating. We do really care for each other.

Todd:

✗ Outside sex has really gotten in the way of the relationship because it's caused conflict. On the other hand, I don't think I could stay in the relationship if it wasn't allowed to continue. Although maybe I would find that I could.

Ron:

✗ It's had a destructive impact. It's been problematic and has caused a lot of hurt on both sides. It's diminished our relationship and has been hard on both of us. During the times when outside sex has worked, I've found it enriching and it has recharged my sexual appetite with Todd.

Connor:

✗ It's brought a real negative to our sex life because of the fear of disease There's more tension. It definitely feels like something has been lost, due to trust and lack of intimacy. We discuss it but there are still things to work out.

Logan:

✗ It's been hurtful. It's caused distrust. I haven't regained my trust in Connor yet, although some of that is about the way we went about it and the way I found out.

Positive impact

The vast majority (75%) of responses were solely positive. We would expect a fairly strong endorsement given participants' self-selection into the study. It's not surprising to us that participants appreciate having a sanctioned sexual outlet. What is striking is the number of benefits beyond having a sexual outlet that participants shared. These included greater communication, increased trust and openness between partners, and the opportunity for individuals to explore and meet individual needs.

Beneficial Impact – Key Themes

(Study participants naming this as a significant impact)

78%	Sanctioned Sexual Outlet
48%	Stimulates Our Sex Life, e.g. titillating, energizing
40%	Different Needs Met
34%	Brought Friends, New Experiences into relationship
33%	Encourages & Reinforces Honesty
27%	Provides Variety, Sense of Freedom
26%	Brought Perspective & Greater Appreciation
24%	Encouraged Sexual Growth (expertise, repertoire, awareness)
23%	Increased Intimacy & Commitment
20%	Encouraged Personal Growth
15%	Wouldn't Be Together Without It

Sanctioned sexual outlet

The first theme was the most basic. Overtly and consciously opening up the relationship, allows couples to pursue outside sex without being deceitful. 78% of the study participants named this as a significant impact.

Having an open relationship is much more satisfying. I hated the pattern of sneaking around – it's a demeaning way to live. If you're not satisfied being monogamous, it's much more healthy psychologically to be open. Having a 'secret life' is tough on everybody – yourself, your partner, and those with whom you play.

It's just sex. It's an outlet. It's neither positive nor negative. But it's important that it's honest.

Having it open works for us. It's way better than lying about it. Thinking it won't happen is a recipe for disaster. We're men. It's like "You really don't expect me not to get a blow job when I need one, do you?"

It takes so much of the worry and the stress and the jealousy away from the relationship. It makes the relationship so enjoyable. It's been awesome.

Sex is really important. I would not have had a happy life if I had tried to damp down that part of my life to be a dutiful little housewife. We both require a lot of sex with a lot of men and we both like it so we have to give each other space. It's just an element of our lives. The fact that it works reinforces it.

It's been a good thing. It keeps things exciting sexually. We still have good sex together after 12 years. We've made some good friends. If we were monogamous, I'd be cheating for sure and if I wasn't, I'd become resentful over time. I'd be resentful of the lack of trust - that I couldn't be trusted to see someone only once. That's what happened in my last relationship.

It's made it much easier for me to handle being away from each other. It would have been hard not having any sex – I have a high libido. It's helped me want to sustain the relationship even though we're separated at times.

It's made us much stronger. It's eliminated the arguing and worrying and tension that there's going to be someone else down the road. It's basically not an arguing point. It takes the pressure off of us sexually, especially when I'm travelling. It makes our other time together that much more precious.

Being open about outside sex makes it so much more comfortable. There's no tension and stress of 'playing the game' of being monogamous. It's been very refreshing. I know he's going to be there for me and so I can play around. I saw him making out with a guy at a party. It was awkward, but I didn't feel jealous because I knew he was going home with me.

Men are wired to like variety and differences. It's an acknowledgement of how we're wired sexually that we can go out together. We have an outlet for this with clear boundaries that allows us to meet those needs honestly and cleanly.

It eliminates the dishonesty and allows us to follow our natural inclinations. I don't think it affects our emotional intimacy. We're avoiding the deceit, mistrust and drama that sometimes comes with this territory.

Stimulates our sex life

48% of study participants shared that having outside sex was helpful to the couples' own sex life. We discussed aspects of this earlier in the sections on Integration and Couples' Own Sex Lives. Here are a few more examples:

It supplements are own sex life. It adds variety. We're sexual beings and it allows for that. It's an ego boost – others still find me attractive. It makes me proud when others find Robert attractive. "He's my man, so that's an ego boost as well.

When you're as horny and provocative as we are, there has to be a sexual outlet. It serves as a release valve. It's not the most important part of our relationship. We have sex together once or twice a week. If I didn't have sex with Gary alone, why would I want to share him with a third? But the outside sex helps break up the patterns that get established and it adds to our repertoire. We often talk about three-ways during sex. We sometimes watch our own movies (with others), while we have sex. If anything it strengthens our relationship.

It helps our sex life to have outside sex. Usually after we're done playing with someone, we end up playing with each other. It turns us on a lot.

It's made the relationship more honest and strong and sometimes livelier. We're not bored with sex. We're not going behind each other's backs. We enjoy playing together. It's above board. It validates how strong the relationship is and after 20 years, you need a little diversity to stoke your interest.

It's improved our sex life. A few years ago, I wasn't as excited at home. I'm not into anonymous sex so our sex life matters. I'm more interested in sex than I would be at this point in my life and it breaks us out of our sexual routines and patterns. We bring new options back.

It makes me happy to see him have a smile on his face. He draws me in and it draws us closer. We're aroused with each other after we've gone out. I'm astounded by how many people comment on how happy we are around each other. They're surprised at how light-hearted we are together. They ask, "Don't you ever get tired of each other?' But we don't.

I've learned more about John's sexual needs and I would never have found out, which means I might never have satisfied him sexually. Going outside augments my need for sex. For both of us, it increases our own self image and confidence. It's fun. It brings more overall sexual satisfaction into my life. It's made us stronger and will continue to make us stronger. I wish we would both have more outside sex. Neither of us is very impulsive.

Different needs met

40% valued outside sex as a way of exploring and meeting differing needs. Differing needs included different types of sex and amount of sex. This was a helpful mechanism in relationships where one partner was struggling with health issues, low libido or significant age differences.

Prostate problems have taken away my sex drive. It's helped that my partner can go out sexually. It relieves my guilt and takes off some of the pressure.

It's been pretty good for us. We don't have sex as often as I would want, so it takes some of the pressure off of both of us. It makes things easier – makes me feel at ease. Thierry is older. His libido is less and he has some health issues which affect his erections, so it keeps me from getting resentful.

We're 28 years apart. My libido is very low and I realize his is much higher. The important thing to me is he is having fun.

Having Jimmy really helped take care of Don's sexual needs, so that was very helpful to me.

We get needs met that wouldn't get met. If one person wants more sex, they can go get it. If we're apart, we can still have sexual lives.

We used to both be versatile, but I've become a top. When we travel, I know it's an opportunity for Gil to find a bottom he can top.

I think the outside relationships have taken the pressure off of Jerry. I have fewer control issues now. No one person could meet all my needs. Jerry isn't into leather so there's no way I could be having the type of S/M sex and relationships I have with him.

It's given us the opportunity to do other things that we wouldn't get to do or experience. I have two Sons and two Dads. Max is into bondage. I'm into breath control.

It breaks the monotony of the relationship – it's exciting. It allows me to get my desire for raw anonymous sex met.

It's an insurance policy. It relaxes things when you can get your needs met elsewhere. I don't think we can be totally responsible for meeting each other's sexual needs. Being able to go out makes our relationship more stable, as it allows each of us to be responsible for our own needs.

Brought friends and new experiences into the relationship

34% talked about finding new friends and discovering new experiences as a result of opening the relationship.

By being open, we experience other people that we wouldn't otherwise know. It enriches the relationship. Some of our best friends we met through outside sex.

Playing outside has widened our circle of friends, made getting intimate with good friends possible, and continually put our own relationship into perspective.

Having boys allowed us to be parents (a surrogate parenting role) and have the experience of being a family. It made us closer to each other because we would work together as a team.

Will's roving libido has been difficult. But it also brought people and experiences into our relationship. Morris was an amazing person. I wouldn't have been at the sex party last weekend and had a fabulously good time if Morris hadn't entered our lives. More importantly, Morris was able to instruct Will about the importance of playing safely. Will couldn't hear that from me.

The reason I wanted an open relationship is because I was exploring S/M and the leather world. It wasn't having sex per se, but I wanted to be able to get naked and experiment. It became a big part of both our identities for a number of years. We got better at communication because of the outside leather sex. We learned to say what we want and don't want, to set limits and to respect boundaries.

We've got some really good friends we have sex with and we've met really neat people through them. It's widened our circle.

Encourages and reinforces honesty

A certain degree of honesty is prerequisite for having an explicit agreement about outside sex. And for the agreement to work, on-going candor is required. 33% reported that having an open relationship encouraged honest conversation about attractions, fears, insecurities, desires – all of which might be easier to not acknowledge.

It's made us honest with each other. We're doing what we want. If we weren't honest about what we wanted, my head would explode.

It's also created a much more honest and trusting environment. Our communication has improved tremendously. We say what we really feel and are comfortable doing it.

It has caused us to look at ourselves and our relationship in a more honest and real way. If we can be honest about this, it makes other stuff easier to be honest about.

Because we opened up the relationship, it makes it stronger. The honesty that's required strengthens our relationship. We've learned to be honest about our needs and to talk more openly about desires toward others without taking offense.

One couple we spoke with waited 24 years before addressing the fact that they were both going out. They described it as a watershed moment and when we spoke with them two years later, they were still excited about how this had changed their interactions. They found themselves being much more honest and open with each other - not only about sex, but also in sharing their respective inner experiences – thoughts, feelings, goals. This level of sharing was new to them and encouraged a much greater intimacy.

It was romantic and monogamous at the beginning. Then we fell into having outside sex, but neither of us ever talked about it. A couple of years ago, we decided to be brutally honest with each other. It's improved because we never used to talk about anything. Now we talk more as individuals. Advice I would give to a new couple: It's better to be honest from the start and just accept someone. Sit down and put your cards on the table. Talk about what you need and don't pretend. Start now, rather than wait 26 years. It's a very freeing experience. When it's not in the open, you know something is happening in the shadows and that's what fuels the insecurity and jealously. You have to realize you can't meet all your partner's needs – you have to meet your own needs.

Provides variety, sense of freedom

27% of participants valued the sense of freedom and/or the variety going outside offered:

I still find Charles very attractive and we have plenty of sex together, but it would have been hard for me not to have sex with anyone else. I would have felt trapped. It would have been like a prison. I would have been able to comply, but I would have been resentful – like there was something out there I wasn't getting to experience.

It's been positive. Although we are devoted to each other, we want to maintain our individuality. It gives us some freedom. We don't want one person to be controlling or dominant. And this goes along with not limiting the other person. Love is about opening up to someone, not controlling them.

It's given us a release valve. Having a life partner doesn't necessitate denying the desire for others. By having permission, you recognize the desire and work together with your partner to accommodate outside sex in a way that is respectful to each other. By having a release valve, it allows us to be closer. It's also helped us loosen some inhibitions.

It gave us wiggle room. Wiggle room to have a little bit of freedom and not be solely dependent on each other.

Having the option to play has allowed us to not feel trapped or caged in the relationship. We haven't had to feel limited or give up the possibility of ever going out. Clark doesn't want to feel controlled or on a leash and this gives him a sense of freedom. And that's true for both of us.

We like variety. I love sex with Will and love making love to Will, but I also like variety. It spices up our sex life.

It relieves frustration. If I'm in a rut, I can go get laid and come home happy. If I come home happy, it helps the relationship. Letting Robert have outside sex makes him bearable. He's so intense; it makes him easier to be with.

On my night out, after outside sex, I can't wait to come home and sleep with Robert.

Brought perspective and greater appreciation

26% of participants talked about the perspective that going outside has brought.

It's helped me realize that there are many aspects to relationship and sex isn't and shouldn't be the primary aspect. Sex may be a relatively minor element in some primary relationships.

I learn a lot by contrasts. Going outside makes me realize what I have in my relationship. Over the years, it's allowed me to see aspects of our relationship and the whole of our relationship and where sex fits in. It's no longer the forbidden fruit.

On the whole it's been positive. We handle each other better. We learned to ask each other more questions – to pull each other out. It carried over beyond sex. We became more aware of each other's needs and became more sensitive. Over the years it helped us appreciate each other more. Sometimes fucking someone else just put things in perspective. Coming home to Dennis was the best thing of the evening.

It continues to strengthen our bond and our appreciation of each other.

It has a positive effect. It adds some life to things; takes you outside the ordinary. It brings variety – like going on vacation. It makes me appreciate the sex and the relationship I have with Max.

It makes us realize the grass is no greener.

It makes us appreciate our relationship, physically and emotionally. It keeps us from being distracted by others. It's a release valve. If it wasn't open, we'd probably both be cheating.

Encouraged sexual growth

24% of participants acknowledged growing sexually as a result of outside experiences. This included increasing their expertise, repertoire and sense of sexuality.

It's helped me become less repressed. I feel like I'm healthier sexually - I'm more relaxed, adventuresome and happier.

Over time it allowed us to experiment and evolve sexually. I was a total top and I've become more versatile.

It's allowed us to be honest about who we are and what we want.

I used it as an opportunity to explore what I had always fantasized about – BDSM. I've learned about myself. I've had a lot of interesting experiences that I wouldn't have had otherwise.

It's made me more aware of my body and my own sexuality. Outside sex is a healthy thing for us and doesn't have any downsides. It has led to our growth as individuals and to the growth of our relationship.

I like to get to walk the world as a sexual being. I like that I haven't had to give that up. Having outside sex and the possibility of outside sex brings excitement.

I'm more comfortable with my sexuality. I had never been to a sex club before. We've gone twice. Once was really good and once was really boring. I don't have any judgments about that kind of thing now. I did before. I'll try new things and I have freedom and also a sense of relief.

Increased intimacy and commitment

23% of participants spoke specifically about intimacy and about the relationship becoming stronger.

It's allowed a deeper intimacy and a deeper relationship. To really be this open requires an enormous amount of integrity, self-confidence and deep honesty. Our experience of having this freedom is indicative of a healthy relationship, not unhealthy. Friends often don't understand the depth of our love and the depth of the relationship because they see us going out and think that that somehow means we care less.

It has helped solidify our relationship. It prompted deeper conversations than we even knew we were prepared to have. It required more sharing at a deeper level.

It encourages us to be more honest about our thoughts and feelings. We're closer with each other. I'm more willing to share 100% of myself with him and there's much less 'mine/yours' & more 'ours'. I find myself more generous – even with finances. I think that's because there's greater trust and I'm happier about the relationship so I want to be more generous.

It's another step on the ladder, another defining point of our commitment. Something we can do together and enjoy doing together that has built our relationship further and made it stronger.

It's enhanced our intimacy. We can have variety by going outside, but it makes me appreciate what we have at home. I equate it to filet mignon. I want to have rib or sirloin, but when I do it makes me appreciate I have filet mignon at home. It's reassuring to be desired. It helps my self-esteem. We're still sexual, a part of the community, feel vital.

We currently have a beautiful man we've taken under our wing. It keeps that fire burning in us. It's amazing how life can open up and what the universe has to show us when you're as connected and in love as we are.

Encouraged personal growth

20% talked more generally about how they had grown personally as a result of outside sexual experiences.

It's created better dynamics in our relationship. I'm more honest with my emotions and able to communicate them. Tom is more self-aware and able to acknowledge that he's made a mistake. He would never have said he was sorry before. I would not have expected it, but being open is far better than it was before. It's made me more in touch with Tom and made me a better person.

We're both on different paths and learning new things. We share with each other what we've learned and we experience the ways each of us has grown. I think eventually we will come back and be more focused on each other sexually with everything we have learned. I would like that and want that . It's made us continually define our relationship – which keeps it alive and growing.

I've asserted myself more in the relationship as a result of having to stick up for the 'rules'. Friends tell me how much I've changed. It's caused us to be much more open and honest.

If we hadn't opened the relationship, I wouldn't have found S/M and that let me grow and become more confident. And my ability to express it and have James support it and support me, increased our intimacy together. James was encouraging and non-judgmental. It's brought us closer.

It's been transformative, although it's a constant balancing and juggling. I've discovered things about myself. I've become connected to new people. It's opened me to new worlds. It's not all positive, but it's made me wiser and I understand that relationships can operate on multiple levels.

It makes us more loving toward each other. It's like exercise. When I'm with someone I'm practicing being loving and I bring it back. The more love I give away the more I have to give.

Outside sex has helped me grow as a person – psychologically, spiritually and lovingly.

Wouldn't be together without it

15% of participants responded rather matter-of-factly that they wouldn't be together without it. This comment was offered in two ways. Some participants felt outside sex was essential and they couldn't imagine going without. Others felt their relationship was essential and they were glad that the lack of sex at home was not a deal-breaker.

It's allowed us to stay together in a great relationship, even though we're not sexually very compatible. If we didn't go out, we'd get frustrated. I'm certain we would break up.

If it hadn't been open, our relationship wouldn't have become long-term. I like variety. "I love you, but there's lots of men out there." Barry is more nurturing and wouldn't have needed outside sex. I needed a long leash and this relationship allowed that.

It has kept us together. I don't want to be celibate or have severe limitations. I'm glad that there are alternatives and I can get my needs met without threatening the relationship.

The relationship wouldn't have survived without it. We like sex with other guys. It's something we both really enjoy. I love to watch him with someone and he loves to watch me with someone. We don't have sex with just each other that much - maybe once a month. We like to have others involved.

Discussion of Results

Providing a descriptive picture of what non-monogamy looks like was a core aim of this study. Because of this, we've stayed very close to the data, providing concrete examples and avoiding speculation. When we step back and look more generally at the study findings, the conclusions we draw are more sweeping.

A viable option

We assume we had a study population skewed towards the positive, but nonetheless, it is reasonable to conclude that non-monogamy for gay male couples is a viable option. When partners find enough common ground in their inclinations and perspectives toward non-monogamy, sanctioned outside sex is a sustainable and satisfying possibility.

If a couple is willing to be forthright and to problem-solve as needed, non-monogamy isn't by nature de-stabilizing. In fact, the results of this study would suggest the opposite – many study couples said non-monogamy enabled them to stay together. The average length of relationship for interviewed couples was 16 years – double our minimum requirement. Given the difficulties we had in recruiting participants, this figure suggests a positive correlation between longevity and non-monogamy. At a minimum, it destroys the myth that opening the relationship is the 'beginning of the end'.

The study also counters a second, and corollary, myth: open relationships are somehow less – less healthy, less loving, less responsible. Again, the results of this study would suggest quite the opposite. Certainly, non-monogamous couples can be as dysfunctional as monogamous couples, but they can also be as nurturing, trusting and cohesive. The vast majority of our study couples appeared to have caring, loving, and healthy partnerships.

What's the payoff?

We found many couples had a somewhat compartmentalized perspective and approach to outside sex. "It's just sex" – a release without meaning, quite separate from the relationship. For these couples, non-monogamy offers a valuable and satisfying outlet that's sanctioned and acknowledged. It allows men to 'follow their nature', meet differing needs, and seek variety without jeopardizing their relationship.

A majority of study couples had a more integrative approach to non-monogamy. There was less anonymity and more personal connection with outside sex partners, more sharing of information and discussion of what got stirred up, and an effort to bring back and utilize the energy and lessons of the outside experience for the betterment of the relationship. For these couples, non-monogamy brought additional benefits beyond the sexual outlet. Couples spoke of greater trust, more forthright communication, personal growth, increased perspective, and more drive in their own sex lives together.

What's the catch?

Some couples experienced non-monogamy as a 'no-brainer'. They found an approach that worked for them with little difficulty or fanfare. This was more likely to be the case if outside sex was agreed upon at the beginning of the relationship and they had a compartmentalizing approach to outside sex.

However, for most couples, there was a price of admission. Non-monogamy came with risks and required maintenance. It may trigger uncomfortable feelings; it may provoke disagreements and tension, it may require self-reflection and personal growth, it may necessitate changing how a couple communicates and interacts. This was especially true for couples that valued sharing and integrating the experiences of non-monogamy. We also suspect this might be more likely for couples in the general population – couples who might be reluctant to participate in a study.

Couples have to decide what will work for them and how they can best minimize and navigate the risks. There isn't a simple model to follow. Couples don't know ahead of time what will surface or what will be required. They may be challenged by any, and probably many, of the following:

- clarifying values and making certain they are mutual,
- appreciating and accommodating differences,
- holding steadfast to agreements and a commitment to honesty,
- growing greater capacity to process and manage their own emotional reactions
- learning to voice their desires, concerns, and uncomfortable feelings
- becoming increasingly vulnerable, trusting, forgiving, generous
- partnering to constructively problem-solve and find resolution for unforeseen and possibly highly charged issues

It's an intriguing list - not advised for the faint-hearted, yet full of possibilities for individual and relationship growth. As one study participant said, "Both people have to want it bad enough to be willing to pay the price and do the work required."

What Is enough communication?

Many couples mentioned that communication was critical. Some couples were very self-reflective and very verbal in their processing. Some couples were deeply in tune with each other and preferred finding their way intuitively. In between were couples that seemed more sporadic or 'hit and miss' in their communication with each other. We were surprised at the number of times

we heard, "Mmmm, we've never discussed that." Or "That's an interesting question, I never really thought about that."

We found ourselves wondering and sometimes worrying about these couples. When they took the initiative to communicate, it worked well for them. But they often defaulted to making assumptions without confirming them with their partner. If the assumptions they made proved to be correct (and they often did), they were home free.

But we began to question if the study had a preponderance of 'couples who were lucky'. In the larger population would we see more couples with this approach that had 'guessed wrong'? We certainly heard from some study couples who paid heavily for a previous lack of communication or proactive consideration. We're speculating here, but if a couple wants to minimize the risks inherent in non-monogamy, it seems best to err on the side of checking out assumptions and inquiring into perspectives.

Dealing with differences

The study couples most likely to struggle were ones that were challenged by core differences. Certainly the most difficult situation was when partners differed in their desire to open the relationship. Until they could come to some shared agreement about what they both wanted, couples typically experienced recurring tension and frustration. We assume this is much more prevalent in the larger population which includes couples reluctant to participate in a study.

Another common area of difficulty was partners who had differing preferences for connection. It took partners time to realize the difference and to recognize the innate character of this difference. Initially there's the assumption - "He thinks like me." After a bit of discovery this becomes, "Why doesn't he think like me?" Unfortunately, accommodation and resolution only become possible when there is recognition that both perspectives are valid. At that point partners can shift to "What will we need from each other to make this work?" – a much more fruitful question to be asking.

There are myriad sources of difference that can prove to be problematic. Partners may have strong differences in values, standards, personality traits, and psychological routines. At what point did you begin to see my 'harmless flirting' as 'disrespect'? How much outside sex does it take before it's labeled excessive? Why are you so jealous/insecure/out of control/uptight/insensitive? In most cases, awareness, empathy, legitimization and creative accommodation can bridge the gap, but it's not always easy getting there.

We had very different personalities and very different perspectives on what was appropriate. We tried using rules, but they never seemed sufficient. One of us would get hurt or uncomfortable and we would have long talks and then we would conscientiously revise the rules. But it was more like we were negotiating - our focus was on right and wrong and fairness and compliance.

The breakthrough came when we finally stepped back and seriously considered what we each wanted and needed from the other. Instead of trying to change each other, we created new 'rules' that actually differed for the two of us. Our friends thought we were crazy, but the new rules allowed us both to get our different needs met. Instead of focusing on complying, we realized we actually wanted to honor and support each other's values and needs. I don't know why it took us so long to get there, but things became much easier when we started acting like we were on the same team... It was a few years after that we had this crazy idea that 'somebody' ought to do a study.

So, where's the support?

Most research shows that approximately two-thirds of long-term male couples who have been together for five years or more are honestly non-monogamous (Shernoff,LCSW, 2007). This means a majority of long-term male couples are creating their own unique models – despite societal injunctions. This is remarkable. And it makes us wonder why there isn't more overt support from the gay community. Why is there a reluctance to discuss non-monogamy – particularly in a community that believes in path-finding?

Although some study couples were very transparent about the openness of their relationship, this was not the case for most. As one participant shares:

Having an open relationship feels like a funny way of being in the closet again. Family and friends expect that we're monogamous, and we don't tell them we're not. It's like a secret. When we travel for work or to see family, we leave friends (and colleagues) at 10pm and then we go out. In our community and society, it feels like something huge isn't being talked about or studied or understood.

When we began telling our friends, colleagues and family about this study, it did remind us of 'coming out'. It sometimes triggered dead silences or a polite change of subject. And it sometimes provoked deep, meaningful conversations.

As a community, we know from our own experiences of coming out that visibility and dialogue are critical. If you're bucking societal norms, it helps to have like-minded souls to reassure you that you're not alone. If you're charting a path where there is no roadmap, it helps to have folks who have been there or who can engage with you in your navigating. The study couples who reported having mentors were uniformly grateful.

Prior to initiating this study we encountered our own reluctance to publicly address this issue; we worried that talking about non-monogamy would be seen as jeopardizing the push for gay marriage. In the 4 years we've taken to complete the study, we never once encountered resistance from any group or organization. Perhaps this was a result of flying under the radar, but it also points to our own internalized fears of speaking about a taboo subject.

Ironically, when California legalized gay marriage (however briefly), we began hearing more and more of our study participants mention their marriages. This wasn't something we tracked, but a majority of the study couples from that point forward spoke of being married. Clearly they weren't equating marriage with monogamy! So,

as a gay community, if we don't want to replicate the heterosexual divorce rate, we might begin looking for ways to talk more openly about how our relationships really work.

We hope this study opens the door to more candid discussions of responsible non-monogamous relationships. We strongly encourage others to research this topic to more thoroughly document:

- the wide range of behavior and choices being made
- the diversity of approach due to race, ethnicity, class and geography
- the generational perspectives
- the respective values of both monogamous and non-monogamous relationships.

In Conclusion

We think this study illustrates and validates the experience many male couples are having. It will be important to ascertain to what degree this kind of information is useful to non-monogamous couples, to couples considering non-monogamy, and to the larger community.

We'd like to end with our appreciation. Many, many thanks to the 86 couples who gave their time and perspective to this study!

— Blake Spears & Lanz Lowen
www.thecouplesstudy.com

Creating Healthy Open Relationships

Lanz Lowen and Blake Spears

One of the reactions to our study, Non-Monogamy in Long-term Male Couples was that people were pleased we brought some light to the subject of male couples in open relationships and made the topic discussable. The descriptions of the various configurations and approaches to non-monogamy seemed to validate the respective directions that readers had taken in their own relationships.

We also received questions and requests for more information. These usually fell into two camps.

- **Camp #1**: What's the best approach, e.g. How can we create an open relationship so that it will work for us? Clearly, there's no single right way. Having said that, we do think there are key elements and behaviors that can help you successfully navigate this terrain. In this article, we share those with you.

- **Camp #2**: How do you handle Issue XYZ, e.g., What do we do about jealousy? Again, there are no cut and dry answers, but we can share insights and examples that we received from study participants that might help couples deal with specific issues.

Creating A Supportive Foundation

If you're having difficulties in your relationship – such as you're getting bored, you've become distant, you argue all the time, or you think your partner is cheating on you – this is not the time to decide to open the relationship. To the contrary, the more solid the relationship, the better the communication, the clearer partners are about their respective values, the more likely non-monogamy can flourish. As a therapist once told us, "if you want an open relationship, recognize that you're upping the ante – it brings risk and requires work." So, one way to think about non-monogamy is to consider the strength and health of your relationship. If you've been together a long time, how satisfied are you with the patterns you've created? If your relationship is fairly new, how are you paying attention to the norms as you create your relationship?

We recently attended a two-day workshop on the research findings of Richard & Julie Gottman, PhD., which are based on extensive longitudinal observation and interview research on couples for many years. They approach their research from the perspective of what can be learned from couples where the relationship is working and how that is different from the couples where the relationship is problematic.

One of the most convincing findings and a core component of their therapeutic interventions is the observation that a healthy couple requires a foundation of pervasive positive regard in which to flourish. The Gottmans found that there needs to be a ratio of 5 positive comments/gestures/invitations for every negative volley. This doesn't mean that a couple doesn't fight or have negative experiences, but even during conflict, a healthy couple often brings forward a positive emotional regard.

According to the Gottmans, this foundation of positive regard is built primarily in three ways. First, couples take an interest in knowing, understanding and appreciating their partner's internal experience and inner world. Each is curious about his partner's daily events, likes and dislikes, upbringing and family, desires, needs, and evolving perspectives on each other, life, and the relationship. We imagine showing interest and curiosity as 'Relationships 101', but the Gottmans observed many couples who no longer updated this information - who no longer asked open-ended questions to know what their partner was feeling, experiencing or thinking.

Secondly, the foundation of positive regard is cultivated by the sharing of fondness and admiration. Expressions of love, affection, and support mattered. Rather than scanning the environment for what is problematic and what they don't like, a healthy couple tends to notice what their partner does right and what they admire. This routine habit of noticing the glass half-full builds a culture of appreciation and respect.

In our study of long-term non-monogamous couples, we found the sharing of fondness and admiration to be most obvious in the 15% of couples who no longer had sex together. The 15% cluster was still actively sexual outside the relationship, but had lost desire within it. In many cases, the couple had never been that sexually compatible. What these couples were clear about is how loving, caring and appreciative they felt toward each other. The common sentiment was, "Why would we want to give up a relationship that brings us so much joy, comfort, companionship and love, just because the sex isn't any good?" They spoke glowingly about their joint ventures, intermingled families, renovated apartments, and their desire to cuddle, express their love, and celebrate their relationship. Although it was not one of our Study questions, this group was the most likely to share that they had been legally married or had created a commitment ceremony to affirm their love.

In our minds, they demonstrated the power of the Gottmans' observations. Sexual needs and , and in some cases emotional ones were being met outside the relationship, but this wasn't undermining, jeopardizing or lessening the connection between the partners. These couples were quick to express their love and appreciation and their happiness with each other was readily apparent.

The third component of the foundation is a bias for turning towards connection, rather than away from it. In everyday moments, partners make bids for emotional connection. They might drop a hint about feeling disappointed, give a minor compliment to their partner, or inquire about the status of an activity that was important to them. To the extent their partner picks up on this and responds favorably, they move closer. Popular movies and television programs that focus on emerging relationships are often built around the missed opportunities for connection. The dramatic tension or situational humor comes from watching a character reach out in hopes of reciprocation, particularly if that gesture is not noticed or not met in some positive way. It is these many small choice points – opportunities for creating a positive foundation - that shape a relationship's course toward health or away from it.

These three components, and the resulting foundation of positive regard, create a momentum toward greater connection. This momentum, and its accompanying beliefs, increase the likelihood of positive outcomes. It's a bit like the dynamic of Self-Fulfilling Prophecy. When there is a belief that goodness and resolution and repair are possible, and likely, it increases the odds of this happening. Bob Weiss calls it the PSO – Positive Sentiment Override. If partners are more likely to notice what's working, assume good intent, and skew their interpretations of comments and interactions to the positive (PSO) then chances for resolution are much greater. When Positive Sentiment Override is operating, misunderstandings are likely to be aired and forgiven.

On the other hand, if a foundation of positive regard has not been built, there may exist NSO – Negative Sentiment Override, in which neutral or even positive messages are perceived negatively. When Negative Sentiment Override is operating a person becomes hyper-vigilant -- primarily noticing the negative, and interpreting the incoming data negatively, resulting in a bias away from connection. The small opportunities for positive connection are squandered, scorching the relationship, rather than breathing life into it.

Partners in our Study demonstrated the elements of a foundation of positive regard, and we in turn observed Positive Sentiment Override. In separate interviews, even when talking about difficulties, they spoke respectfully and admiringly about their partners. They described different perspectives fairly, acknowledging the conflict in their viewpoints and being careful to represent their partner's perspective accurately. We think their tendency toward PSO and their supportive foundations helped them be more capable of successfully navigating the challenges and unknowns that come with non-monogamy.

Honoring Differences

Some of the couples in our study had no issues whatsoever with non-monogamy. They both wanted an open relationship and had similar ideas about how it should work. Furthermore, they were both wired similarly in their preferred approach, e.g. they both enjoyed anonymous outside sex, thought it was essential, yet thought it was no big deal. Or they both valued intimacy with others and were disinclined to be competitive, insecure, or jealous.

However, the majority of couples in our study were not so lucky. Many of their differences in personality, self-esteem, familial patterns, and core values had an impact on their approach to being non-monogamous. For these couples, becoming aware of differences and managing those differences was essential.

We hypothesize that managing differences is a continuum. There's an assumption of sameness on one end of the continuum and being fully supportive of those differences on the other end. (See graphic below). Couples in the Study reported their experiences in various stages.

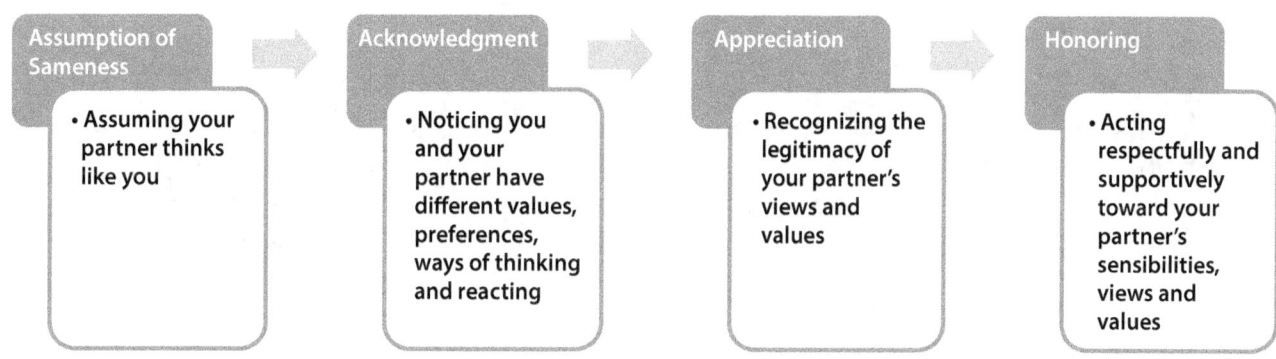

Assumption of Sameness	Acknowledgment	Appreciation	Honoring
• Assuming your partner thinks like you	• Noticing you and your partner have different values, preferences, ways of thinking and reacting	• Recognizing the legitimacy of your partner's views and values	• Acting respectfully and supportively toward your partner's sensibilities, views and values

Russ and Terry

Russ and Terry assumed they were alike even though they came from very different backgrounds. Russ had been married for many years prior to partnering with Terry and was relatively new to the gay scene. On the other hand, Terry had come out in college, remained single and had been sexually active most of his adult life. When Russ and Terry agreed to open their relationship, Terry enthusiastically talked Russ into going to a sex club. Terry loved anonymous sex, the thrill of the chase, having multiple partners, and lots of variety. Russ assumed he would like it too and was up for the experience. However, as Russ reported later, "I hated it! It felt cheap and degrading and I didn't want to have sex with people I didn't know. And I wasn't comfortable trying to hook up. Everyone looked better than me and there seemed to be rules about what was supposed to happen. I went one more time, but then I told Terry, 'Never again'. "

Russ and Terry had discovered important differences in what they preferred and valued. It turned out that getting to know someone was an essential part of sex for Russ – a prerequisite. Having discovered their differences, they were both sufficiently mature to acknowledge both perspectives and began figuring out ways they could meet their respective needs. However, they soon realized that neither of them was fully accepting of the other's approach. Russ couldn't understand how Terry could want to have sex that he deemed 'degrading' and Terry discovered he was more 'okay' with the idea of Russ having anonymous sex more than he was with Russ having sex and relationships with real people.

One of the things they said that helped them was talking to an older couple that had a lot of experience and validated both perspectives. Over time, Russ learned to understand Terry's perspective - it was all play and fantasy to Terry.

On Terry's side he found he actually went too far in accommodating Russ. Russ befriended Albert, who initially became a close friend of Russ's and then became close to both Russ and Terry. Terry liked Albert and occasionally the three of them would have sex, but over time it became clear that the energy was primarily between Russ and Albert. Terry realized he wasn't comfortable with this and when the relationship ended, Russ and Terry established a new agreement, "You can fuck whomever you want, but you can't take him out to dinner."

This resolution seemed to be working for them at the time of the interviews. Both perspectives were seen as legitimate and both partners were acting in ways that were supportive of those differences (while still respecting their own needs and being protective of the relationship).

Mike and Luis

Mike and Luis knew they were wired very differently. They worked hard at their relationship, yet despite good communication and good intent, they often found themselves arguing about outside sex. When a problem arose, there would be hurt feelings, defensiveness, and then a constructive effort to revise 'the rules' so that 'it wouldn't happen again'. Unfortunately, "No matter how many times we modified the rules, Mike found a way to bend them" (according to Luis).

They're big shift came one day when they were talking about their new tattoos. Mike had a huge Eagle with wings spread across his back and Luis had a magnificent lion prowling through his chest hair. The two tattoos were significant. For Mike, the Eagle represented freedom – the ability to fly anywhere he wanted. For Luis, the Lion was about strength, pride and security – having a place where he knew he was King. While talking about the significance of the tattoos, they began relating their tattoos to their sexual proclivities and found themselves arguing familiar territory. Luis wanted to be able to go to the gym and not run into any of Mike's 'fuck-buddies'. He wanted his home and surroundings to be sacred. Security was important to him and surprises were jarring.

Mike, on the other hand, didn't care who Luis fucked or where he ran into them. He just wanted the freedom to play with others and to do it without feeling secretive or 'getting in trouble'. Luis wanted to own his territory and Mike wanted to fly above the radar.

At this point, it occurred to them that if a Lion and an Eagle are fundamentally wired so differently than maybe they needed different rules from each other. Their solution: Luis could do whatever he wanted sexually and play wherever he wanted (Mike wasn't bothered by much and he knew Luis would always be respectful). Mike, on the other hand, would agree to only play when he was traveling for work (unlike Luis's job, Mike's job required a fair amount of travel). What Mike did while he was traveling was his business, although they still had rules about emotional involvement that applied equally to both of them.

By creating separate rules, Mike and Luis were fully legitimizing each other's perspectives for the first time. They had been so busy trying to legislate fairness that they were losing sight of how to respectfully appreciate their corresponding differences. Mike realized he had never fully accepted Luis's position as legitimate. He was caught in the trap of "Why is Luis so 'old school'? (Why isn't he enlightened like me?)." Luis, on the other hand, had always been quick to denigrate Mike's desire for freedom because it trampled on his own desire to be secure in the place where he lived. Luis couldn't understand how Mike could have so little respect for his sensibilities.

...cont'd next page

The new rules were helpful, but their new thinking had an even greater impact. It occurred to Mike that he wasn't really seeing Luis as a Lion, but merely focusing on the ways he wasn't an Eagle. The absurdity of not respecting the needs (and strengths) of a Lion was startling. Mike began to really appreciate Luis's views and he realized for all the years they had been together, he had merely complied with the rules – rules that didn't really make sense to him, although he was clear he wanted to avoid Luis's roar. Mike began operating from a different mindset. He realized the extent to which his freedom-seeking behavior had hurt Luis and he began honoring Luis's needs, rather than minimizing or belittling them.

Luis shifted his perspective as well. He began seeing Mike's needs as legitimate, rather than reckless or uncaring. He noticed Mike's efforts and became more trusting. Ironically, he reported that once he felt like he had more control, he felt freer and in less need of it.

Addressing Conflict

Being able to manage conflict is a core skill required for enduring relationships. Being able to 'fight fair' – constructively discuss an issue without escalating into a cycle of defensiveness, criticism, or contempt is essential. Conflict within a relationship is a given – it may arise from differences in likes/dislikes, interests, personality styles, values and beliefs, and ways of approaching problems. Most therapists and researchers would agree on some version of the following principles:

- Sharing honestly about actions, thoughts and emotions.

- Being able to communicate – ideally verbally – about your emotions, concerns, and needs, even if it makes your partner uncomfortable.

- Avoiding attacks – name-calling, negative attributions, dragging up old wounds, etc.

- Being open to feedback and hearing what might be problematic

- Assuming good intent when constructively addressing an issue

-

- Having the belief that many problems are resolvable, that misunderstandings can be cleaned up, and that constructively airing issues is preferable to ignoring them

Conversely, the Gottmans describe the negative cycle of conflict in terms of the Four Horsemen of the Apocalypse: Criticism, Contempt, Defensiveness, and Stonewalling (see side bar). Any one (or more) of these may make constructive resolution of conflicts considerably more difficult for couples.

Being in an acknowledged open relationship requires good communication. Couples reported that "Being Honest" was the most important characteristic of making non-monogamy work. Negotiated non-monogamy is built upon the principle of truthfully disclosing outside sexual behavior to the level agreed upon by the couple. However, being honest also included acknowledging the desires of which they're aware, their degree of emotional involvement with outsiders, the extent to which they are comfortable or uncomfortable with the non-monogamous arrangement, and the reactions they might have to their partner when they have outside sex or get involved with others.

Four Horsemen

1. Criticism:

Attacking your partner's personality or character, usually with the intent of making someone wrong: ("you always..." "you never..." "you're the type of person who ..." "why are you so ...").

2. Contempt:

Attacking your partner's sense of self with the intention to insult or psychologically abuse him/her: (Insults and name-calling; hostile humor, sarcasm or mockery; sneering or rolling your eyes).

3. Defensiveness:

Seeing self as the victim, warding off a perceived attack: ("Making excuses; Cross-complaining: meeting your partner's complaint, or criticism with a complaint of your own, thereby ignoring what your partner said; Disagreeing and then cross-complaining: "That's not true, you're the one who ..." "I did this because you did that..."; Yes-butting: start off agreeing but end up disagreeing.

4. Stonewalling:

Withdrawing from the relationship as a way to avoid conflict. Partners may think they are trying to be "neutral" but stonewalling conveys disapproval, icy distance, and/or smugness: Silent Treatment; Monosyllabic mutterings; Changing the subject; Leaving the room.

Certainly the skill level of managing conflict varied amongst Study couples. However, we do think a couple that is willing to openly discuss non-monogamy may be more comfortable addressing potential conflict. The willingness to acknowledge personal wants and desires, to hear about what their partner may need or want from someone other than themselves, and to deal with the reactions of their partner as they disclose potentially charged experiences require either a comfort with conflict or a willingness to make oneself and their partner uncomfortable.

On the other hand, we did see a big difference between couples that had an agreement for outside sex, but did not disclose the details of the experiences. These couples were less comfortable with conflict, dealing with each others' reactions and managing their own feelings of jealousy, envy, and vulnerability. The couples that disclosed the most seemed to value articulating and working on relationship issues as a way of resolving them and also learning from them. We can't say that one approach is healthier than another – what's most critical is what is right for the individuals involved. However, couples that disclose and discuss more have more opportunity to learn about themselves and each other, to practice and improve communication skills, and potentially to develop a deeper, more tested trust.

The Gottmans talked about two types of conflict. The first type consists of conflicts around problems that are resolvable – issues that just require clarification, compromise and constructive problem-solving.

This could be something simple like how to decorate a room or something more substantial like whether to buy a house. The thorniest conflicts we heard addressed issues where one partner became too involved with an outsider. A crisis ensued. Trust is shaken. The structure and safety of the partnership feels threatened and partners feel emotionally vulnerable and volatile (hurt, betrayal, fear, jealousy, anger). At these moments good Positive Sentiment Override really pays off. The couples we interviewed were able to work through these times even though they acknowledged that they never wanted to repeat the experience.

To the extent the issue can be constructively discussed, it is usually resolved with a new understanding and a new agreement. For example, Ruben got 'too involved' with an outside partner. Jack insisted he stop seeing the guy and they had several deep discussions about the issue.

Ruben: "I learned I have to manage myself much more carefully. If I find I'm getting too enamored with someone, I make sure we stop having sex or I stop seeing them."

Jack: "Since then, we've had an agreement that I can ask Ruben to stop seeing someone if I think he's getting too involved. I've never had to do that, but I think knowing I could is reassuring."

The second type of conflicts – long-term, intractable issues that are probably not resolvable, but instead require on-going dialogue about the perpetual problem. In type two conflict, in order to avoid gridlock a great deal of positive regard is required even when disagreeing.

In the Study, one of the most memorable conflicts a couple shared was during the AIDS crisis. Both partners were involved in a gay men's spiritual group that valued openness, emotional closeness, a strong sense of caring and community and a certain amount of freedom to dive head-first into personal and spiritual growth. Given the times, the group had lost a number of key members to AIDS and probably 1/3 of the group was dealing with the illness themselves. It was definitely not a time of 'business as usual'. Emotions were raw, members were perpetually grief-stricken, and the old rules about what's a couple, what's an emotional boundary, what's the appropriate amount of emotional distance to keep were all tossed on their head. "When someone is dying and you care about them and they are reaching out for help, you don't want to put barriers in the way of your intimacy." This was a particularly sensitive issue in the gay community where many men with AIDS had been rejected and ostracized by their families.

Larry and Ron

In the midst of this was Larry and Ron. They had an agreement for an open relationship, but with some understanding that they would not get too emotionally involved with any one person. Ron had a penchant for 'falling in love', which he tried to keep in check, but given the circumstances with AIDS, it didn't seem possible or, for that matter, what either Larry or Ron really wanted. They didn't want to jeopardize their relationship, but neither man wanted to see Ron pull away from a partner he adored who was a year or two away from dying. This was an on-going dilemma that required a lot of discussion, experimenting with various rules, and the perseverance to struggle through painful periods of doubt, tension, and sadness.

One of the more creative ways they dealt with their dilemma was to establish the rule that "You can only date the terminally ill." This seemingly macabre and tongue in cheek prohibition was actually serious. The rule implied that what was tolerated under the circumstances of someone dying would not be tolerated under 'normal' circumstances. It was a way of protecting the relationship without restricting the desires and considerations of a crisis situation.

Tim and Rob

Tim and Rob, on the other hand, were less willing to surface conflict. Tim had had surgery for debilitating hemorrhoids and no longer was comfortable having anal sex. Rob missed it terribly. Even though they had agreements to be open, Rob was reluctant to do so. He didn't want to make Tim feel bad about his health and he was a little afraid Tim might react angrily. Most importantly, he wanted this relationship to work and he didn't want to do anything to jeopardize it. Unfortunately, not speaking up didn't do anything to help move the conversation forward or help Rob meet his sexual needs. Tim and Rob may have a type two conflict that doesn't offer an easy solution. As daunting as that may be, their growth, intimacy, capacity to 'fight fairly' and the positive regard they hold for each other could be enhanced by tackling this issue even if they don't find a 'perfect' or permanent solution.

Trust

Trust is an essential ingredient in a healthy couple. It begins with a leap of faith – a willingness to trust the other. When the willingness to trust is not betrayed, the trust builds and deepens. In this sense trust is both an action and an outcome.

In our Study, we heard trust described as an action – "I trust my partner will be honest with me." "I trust that my partner doesn't want to hurt me or see me get hurt." "I trust my partner is committed to making this relationship work."

We also heard about trust as an outcome. "We're more trusting because we went through a bad spell when Richard got too involved with someone. It was a bit of a crisis and we had to work things out. Now that we have, I think we're even more committed and more trusting of one another. I know how much he cares about me and this relationship. We've been tested."

Couples, who permitted emotional connection with outsiders, were more likely to discuss, test, and affirm their trust. More communication was needed and a greater willingness to trust was necessary given that they were taking greater risks by becoming emotionally vulnerable and connected. To the degree they successfully navigated this terrain, their sense of trust in each other deepened. Each experience re-affirmed and reinforced their trust in each other.

John and Les

John and Les were wired very differently. John was an open-hearted adventurer, who was passionately interested in yoga, self-growth, and Eastern religions. Les was introverted, a workaholic who loved his profession, and who was very secure and comfortable in his own skin. Les trusted John to get involved with other men, to become emotionally attached, and to explore their spirituality together. Les was comfortable with John spending the weekend hiking or attending a meditation retreat with whomever John was interested in at the time.

Les felt like John was trustworthy and he couldn't see the point in curtailing John's desire to discover himself and the world. He knew John would be miserable if he couldn't actively explore possibilities and have new experiences. "Basically, I want him to be happy. Right now, he's hanging out with Kip, a very sweet, good looking guy that John finds interesting. They have a lot in common and seem to have great fun together. If I were ever to get jealous or feel threatened, this would be the time. He's John's 'perfect guy' for that part of John that wants to explore psychological growth and spirituality. I have to remind myself of our trust; I check in with John about how he's feeling; And I focus on what's important to me in my life. Although it causes me a bit of concern, I think our relationship is solid. Kip is giving John the things I can't give him and don't want to give him. We've been here before and it all worked out."

David Meister, an authority on trust, identifies the elements necessary for trust in his formula:

$$\frac{\text{Credibility} + \text{Reliability} + \text{Empathy}}{\text{Self-Interest}} = \text{Trust}$$

According to Meister, trust is built primarily by increasing the three elements in the numerator. However, those elements can be seriously diminished by a large denominator. The formula's denominator is 'self-interest' – a partner's focus on their own needs at the expense of the overall needs of the couple. In other words, if Partner A is only looking out for himself, even though he may be reliable and empathetic, Partner B will be less likely to trust him.

Trust Numerator

- Am I behaving responsibly?
- Am I consistently living up to our agreements and the spirit behind them?
- Am I being sensitive to my partner's needs and feelings? Do I really understand and have empathy for the impact I have on my partner?

Trust Denominator

- Am I approaching issues through the lens of us as a couple or am I just looking at things from my own viewpoint? Am I wanting what's best for both of us or am I primarily focusing on getting what I want by being aggressive, strategic or manipulative?

Jerry and Brad

Jerry: "Brad is very honest about his actions and never tries to hide anything. He's good about only having safe sex and I never worry about him getting too emotionally involved. In general he's supportive, willing to listen, and I feel like he's totally in my corner. However, when it comes to outside sex, he's out of control. Brad's got that Bear look that guys love and they're constantly coming on to him. Finding partners is no big deal to him. I'm much less secure about myself and confident about my sexual abilities. I have a hard time meeting guys I feel comfortable with. Brad doesn't take this into consideration. He's frequently cruising guys when we're out together and constantly finding new partners at the gym. It's not like he's overtly doing anything wrong, but he's not the least bit sensitive to how it makes me feel. When he starts flirting or telling me about his latest conquest, I get envious and then start feeling inadequate. We stopped doing 3-ways because I always felt like a 3rd wheel. Lately, I've been withdrawing – I could talk to him about it, but I really don't trust that he will change."

From Jerry's point of view, Brad has some key elements of trust (credibility and reliability; empathy when it doesn't involve sex). However, Brad's self-absorption when it comes to outside sex is undermining Jerry's trust in Brad. In order to improve the level of trust, Jerry will need to be willing to confront Brad and Brad will need to be open to looking at his own behavior and the impact it is having on Jerry and the relationship.

Managing Jealousy

Jealousy is referred to a lot in the literature and it's usually the first concern mentioned by people who aren't in open relationships. We focus on it here because it can be a thorny issue and we use it as a way of summarizing what we have covered.

Despite its reputation, jealousy wasn't brought up by our study participants as often or as heatedly as we expected. Only 21% of couples mentioned jealousy – bringing it up on their own or naming it when we asked about issues. For the majority of the 21%, jealousy was talked about in past tense – as something they had learned to deal with.

A few found it was a matter of just facing it and making a decision. Tom told us, "Early in our relationship it became clear I had to learn to deal with my jealousy if we were going to be a couple. We both wanted an open relationship, but it was my first time. We lived in the heart of the Castro. Steven is very hot, has a huge dick, and he works out of our house. Walking the dog, going to the gym, getting coffee – he was always being presented with opportunities. I got really jealous, but decided if I wanted to be in this relationship – which I really did - I just wouldn't be able to indulge in those feelings. It's like I stopped allowing myself to go there and instead I just focused on my own needs and desires, not his."

Another strategy was used by couples that preferred minimum disclosure. "I don't want to hear what Jerry does. It makes me uncomfortable – both envious and jealous. We don't talk about what we do and as long as I don't see or hear about it, I have no trouble." This strategy seemed to work well for couples with minimal disclosure and agreements or norms that limited outside connection and emotional involvement. Outside sex was kept in a box away from the primary relationship and so the chance of triggering troublesome reactions like jealousy was minimized.

Some participants mentioned jealousy as something they just had to live with and manage constructively when it came up. "Terry sometimes gets jealous. It often surprises me because we've had an open relationship for years. When it happens, I have to slow myself down and make sure I don't dismiss it. I try to reassure him and sometimes he wants that and sometimes he doesn't. He's pretty good about dealing with it, but because he can get jealous, I've learned to be more careful about openly flirting."

3 Steps to Help Manage Jealousy

1 Learn to constructively acknowledge, discuss and explore the issue as they arise. Can the jealous partner learn to describe the feelings without attacking and blaming? Can the partner triggering the jealousy listen without becoming defensive or dismissive? Can both partners move to clarification, exploration and reassurance?

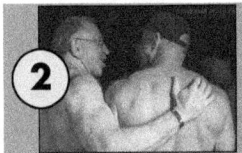

2 Reflect on underlying issues that may be triggering or exacerbating the jealousy. Self-reflection is useful for both partners (see below). Better understanding of the nature of the jealousy provides more options for reassurance, self-growth, and responsible caring behavior.

3 Agree on ways to minimize or limit triggering events and create patterns that are supportive and likely to reduce feelings of volatility, competitiveness, and insecurity.

Barry and Scott

Jealousy can be a multi-headed monster, especially when the foundation of the relationship isn't solid, which was the case with Barry and Scott. Barry complained about feeling very jealous of Scott. "I hate the sight of him kissing another man and I get really upset when I know he might be out fooling around. I imagine he's going to meet someone much more handsome than me and that will be the beginning of the end. When he comes home, I tend to prosecute him to make sure he tells me everything that's happened. He gets really defensive and then gives me the silent treatment. We've been dealing with this for several years – ever since we opened the relationship. We opened the relationship because I discovered Scott was fooling around on the side – Nothing serious, but lots of one-time transgressions that he wasn't telling me about. We split up for awhile and then we decided we would try having an open relationship. It hasn't really worked that well – in fact it seems like it's resulted in a lot of jealousy, hurt feelings and unhappiness on both sides."

If we step back from Barry's comments we can hypothesize that a number of issues might be at work. In addition to the tendency to become jealous, Barry and Scott might also be dealing with:

- Barry's insecurity around his own looks and concerns about how attractive Scott finds him.

- Scott possibly being insensitive, dismissive, and/or disloyal to Barry.

- Unfinished business about Scott fooling around prior to opening the relationship .

- Both partners having difficulty constructively discussing the issue without attacking, defending, or stonewalling.

- Either or both partners having difficulty trusting and being confident about their commitment? Each other's love? Whether or not an open relationship can really work?

Jealousy is the headline, but there are underlying issues and symptoms of a relationship that's on shaky ground. In order to successfully reflect on and address both jealousy and the underlying issues, Barry and Scott might need to:

- <u>Build a stronger foundation of positive regard</u>. Barry and Scott may need to share more, listen more, and ask more questions (as an interested and concerned partner, not as a prosecutor).

They may need to provide more affirmations of each other and the relationship, e.g. feedback about what they appreciate in each other, what they like about the relationship, why they want to be together, feelings of love and connection. Having a bigger emotional bank account will allow them to assume good intent and more quickly repair slights, slips and misunderstandings. A positive foundation will enhance their ability to reassure each other and trust in the relationship and each other.

- Actively honor their differences. They seem to be aware and acknowledging of their differences. It's not clear, however, to what extent they perceive the other's position and inclination as legitimate. Scott needs to be able to really honor Barry's tendency to get jealous and fearful. Honoring means taking Barry's sensibilities into account when having outside interactions – weighing the potential impact his actions may have on the relationship. Honoring means attentively listening even though Scott may not think there's anything for Barry to be worried about. Barry, on the other hand, may need to see Scott's desire for variety as legitimate, not a negative reflection on Barry or an indication of irresponsibility or immaturity.

- Constructively address the conflicts as they arise. This is not a one-time event or something that will be resolved by one heart-to-heart conversation. Scott and Barry need to be able to have a constructive, on-going dialogue about these issues whenever they arise. This requires learning to fight fairly, so when a conflict is triggered they don't descend into a downward cycle of criticism, defensiveness and withdrawal. Things will get said poorly and feelings will be hurt, but they need to learn to repair the damage, re-engage in the dialogue and build their confidence in their ability to do so.

- Actively trust each other and pay attention to the elements crucial for on-going trust. Scott needs to look at his own behavior to identify the ways he might be contributing to the problem. To what extent might he be disregarding Barry's need for loyalty? Acting competitively? Behaving irresponsibly or insensitively or disrespectfully? Barry needs to be able to express his concerns and get reassurance, but then take a leap of faith and trust Scott at his word. To successfully do this, Barry will need to be able to reassure himself, e.g. remind himself that Scott has been truthful for the last 12 months, that Scott has clearly expressed his commitment to the relationship and his behavior is consistent with that, etc. Both Scott and Barry will have to make sure they build track records of living up to their commitments (Is Scott continuing to be forthcoming with facts and avoiding surprises? Is Barry surfacing issues in a constructive manner?) They both will need to be able to empathize with the other. They both will need to take responsibility for 'jointly holding the relationship' ensuring that they are looking through a lens that includes the views and needs of both of them.

Having built a stronger foundation for their relationship, the actual work around managing jealousy will be easier and have a much better chance of success.

Although both partners can react jealously, we mainly heard about situations where one partner was more inclined to become jealous. We assume a person can be predisposed to react in a jealous manner when they are feeling unsafe, insecure, or disrespected. However, this tendency is usually triggered and exacerbated by underlying issues in the relationship that are the responsibility of both parties. Although one partner may be the one inclined to become jealous, the partner triggering the jealousy may have a significant role in creation of the dynamic. Viewing jealousy from a system perspective is more likely to result in positive outcome.

See Sidebars below:

Self-reflection for the jealous partner(s)

○ Is it about him being with anyone else or just someone else to whom I'm attracted?

○ Is it about a particular person? What is it about this person that is threatening?

○ Is it related to my need for loyalty? To what extent am I feeling competitive? To what extent am I feeling possessive? Am I experience him as being: Competitive? Disloyal? Disrespectful of me? Disrespectful of our relationship?

○ Is it related to my confidence in the relationship? Do I have concerns about whether he loves me? Do I have concerns about whether this will jeopardize our relationship?

○ Do I have a belief that he shouldn't need anyone but me? That I should be able to meet all of his needs? That he will leave me if he finds someone better?

○ Is my jealousy related to how I feel about myself? My looks? My confidence?

○ Is it related to my own opportunities? How much of it is envy, rather than jealousy? If I would have had good outside sex yesterday, would that have made a difference? If I had someone hot lined up to play with in the near future, would that make a difference?

○ To what extent am I willing to reassure myself (based on successful history, my trust in our relationship, my trust in my partner's love)? To what extent am I needing reassurance from my partner?

Self-reflection for the triggering partner(s)

○ To what degree do I fully understand and appreciate the impact my outside sexual behavior has on my partner?

○ To what extent am I playing by the rules and the spirit of the rules? Are our agreements overtly clear to both of us?

○ How important is loyalty to me? How important is loyalty to my partner? To what extent am I respectful of his needs for loyalty? To what extent does he feel I'm being respectful of our relationship?

○ Is there any part of me that feels competitive? That enjoys the conquest and showing off the prize? That needs constant validation? That feels compulsive?

○ Am I feeling a need for more attention and appreciation from my partner? Are there needs I'm getting met outside that might be better met with my partner?

○ To what extent am I valuing my partner? Communicating my appreciation? Honoring our differences?

○ Am I keeping my partner informed about my activities in the manner in which he prefers? Am I avoiding surprises? To what extent might I be acting impulsively?

Conclusion

In concluding, we go back to the Study responses about what most helped a couple successfully maintain an open relationship. Two answers stood above the others. The top answer was honesty. Honesty was seen as a prerequisite for everything that followed. A healthy foundation can only be built on truthfulness and the trust that your partner is being truthful.

The second most frequent answer was communication. In this article we've shared what that communication may need to look like. The content of the communication might be quite different in an open relationship, but the need for acknowledging and honoring differences and constructively working to bridge them is no less important. Healthy open relationships are definitely possible, but they require the same conscientious hard work that is needed by all couples trying to build relationships that foster caring, connection, and trust.

Note: We again would like to thank all of the couples who participated in our Study for their time and willingness to be so forthright in detailing the nature of their relationships and their individual feelings.

Bibliography

Non-monogamy in Long-term Male Couples, Blake Spears and Lanz Lowen, 2010. www.thecouplesstudy.com

Bridging the Couple Chasm, John Gottman, PhD and Julie Schwartz Gottman, PhD, The Gottman Institute, Inc., 2011.

The Seven Principles of Making Marriage Work, John Gottman, PhD, Three Rivers Press, 1999.

The Trusted Advisor, David Maister, Charles Green & Robert Galford, 2000.

Blake Spears is a founder and principal of InSight Healthcare and has eighteen years of experience in working with clients in the healthcare industry. Blake conducts research to assess market potential and the positioning of new pharmaceutical products and medical devices in a variety of clinical areas.

Blake has moderated over 150 focus groups and conducted thousands of in-depth interviews with clinicians and opinion leaders. Blake's academic credentials include a B.S. in chemical engineering from Virginia Polytechnic Institute and an MBA from the Stanford Graduate School of Business.

Other Interests:
Blake serves on the boards of the National AIDS Memorial Grove, The HIV Story Project, The Maitri Compassionate Care Foundation, Second Opinion, and the Oakland Mayor's Commission on Aging.

Lanz Lowen coaches executive leaders and facilitates teams in clarifying purpose, defining strategic priorities, resolving conflict, and increasing influence. Coaching engagements, as well as team interventions, typically begin with survey assessments and/or individual interviews. For more information see: (www.mandanagroup.com)

Lanz is an adjunct staff-member at Stanford University's School of Business and at JFK University's Coaching Certificate Program. Prior to establishing his consulting practice, Lanz was the Manager of Organization Development and Training in the corporate offices of Mervyn's Department Stores.

Lanz Lowen has an M.S. in Industrial and Organizational Psychology from San Francisco State and an M.A. in Clinical Psychology from the Professional School of Psychology in San Francisco.

Other Interests:
Lanz was very involved in the early AIDS movement, running volunteer support groups for the AIDS Health Project and creating an independent video profiling long-term survivors (Living Courageously). He is a founding Board Member of Shamanic Circles (www.shamaniccircles.org), an occasional DJ and a dedicated flagger.

www.ingramcontent.com/pod-product-compliance
Lightning Source LLC
Chambersburg PA
CBHW051956280526
45793CB00005B/745